VEXATIOUS TRIFLES

From the writings of Sir Fretful Murmur in his book
MORE MISERIES
ADDRESSED TO: The Morbid, The Melancholy and the Irritable

Edited by Matthew West
Illustrated by Jess Pillings

HIRST publishing

VEXATIOUS TRIFLES

This edition first published November 2010
by Hirst Books

Hirst Books, Suite 285 Andover House, George Yard, Andover, Hants SP10 1PB

ISBN 978-1-907959-00-4

Copyright © Matthew West & Jess Pillings, 2010

The rights of Mr Matthew West to be identified as the author of this work have
been asserted in accordance with the Copyright, Designs and Patents Act 1988.

All rights reserved. No part of this publication may be reproduced, stored in or introduced into a retrieval system, or
transmitted, in any form, or by any means (electronic, mechanical , photocopying, recording or otherwise) without
the prior written permission of the publisher. Any person who does any unauthorised act in relation to this
publication may be liable to criminal prosecution and civil claim for damages

A CIP catalogue record for this book is available from the British Library.

Cover and book design by Mr Robert Hammond

Printed and bound by Good News Digital Books

Paper stock used is natural, recyclable and made from wood grown in sustainable forests. The manufacturing
processes conform to environmental regulations.

This book is sold subject to the condition that it shall be not, by way of trade or otherwise, be lent, re-sold, hired out,
or otherwise circulated without the publisher's prior consent in any form of binding or cover other than that in which
it is published and without a similar condition including this condition being imposed on the subsequent purchaser.

www.hirstbooks.com

www.vexatioustrifles.com

VEXATIOUS TRIFLES

From the writings of Sir Fretful Murmur in his book
MORE MISERIES
ADDRESSED TO: The Morbid, The Melancholy and the Irritable

For Jo

and

Dedicated to the memory of John Stanley Gottrell

The authors offer their grateful thanks to
Mr h for the beautiful design and layout of the book you're
reading right now, Rachel Watkins for her marvellous grasp
of French, Peter West for proofing and general enthusiasm,
Gabriel Woolf for his attention to detail and his beautiful
readings, Richard Westall for his research and infinite patience,
Mike Cook for his dedication to Hirst Books,
and Tim Hirst for so far never saying No.

"Woes cluster – rare are solitary woes
They love a train. They tread each other's heel"

INTRODUCTION.

A few years ago I was plodding around a book fair at Dorking Halls in Surrey. Among the usual tat; dog-eared copies of Robbie Williams' autobiography and endless Ordinance Survey maps – I happened upon a tiny hardback book. It wasn't sitting proudly on display in an alarmed glass cage surrounded by armed guards, nor was it placed respectfully on a velvet cushion surrounded by pot pourri. Instead it was sitting behind some *Blue Peter* annuals stopping the book case from toppling forwards.

The book is essentially the one you hold in your hands, though it has been tidied up and presented respectfully for your modern eyeballs. Written under a clear pseudonym it is perhaps a perfect example of observational comedy from the 1800s.

The tragedy is; none of it is presented as such. It is indeed a seemingly endless list of woes and miseries. Bread and honey to a misanthropic curmudgeon such as myself. Its sense of first-person Schadenfreude appealed to me greatly. It left me feeling that all these things which irritate and annoy me in a day were irritating and annoying someone two hundred years previously.

For a while I tried to paint a portrait of Sir Fretful Murmur. There are clues to the man himself in the introduction and in the Miseries themselves. He is clearly a writer of plays and prose, a singer and pianist, a God-fearing man and unmarried. On this last point one should add that this status is something he strives to improve upon. Barely a Misery goes by without him attempting to make contact with ladies which, one feels, may be (to use a modern parlance) out of his league.

Giles Whimble states in his introduction that he considered tidying up and grammatically improving on Sir Fretful Murmur's original letters. Indeed the temptation is there for me too, some 200 years later. However in doing so it would not do the work justice. Murmur's love of the comma is clear and while on occasions I have made small changes, the rest has been left well alone. My only major change was to number each Misery for ease of reference.

I hope you enjoy these Miseries as much as I do.

Matthew West May 2010, 200 years later.

DEDICATION.

To GEORGE COLMAN, Esq.

Dear Sir,

THOSE who know you, as we do superior beings, by their works only, and those who enjoy the happiness of your friendship, will, no doubt, at first, wonder that a book upon Miseries should be addressed to the Author of Broad Grins, to one whose wit ever brilliant, yet ever amiable, has so often augmented the felicities of life: but they will immediately perceive how closely you are connected with my dismal subject, then they reflect upon the misery which you frequently occasion; as the Curtain descends upon your Drama, as they reach the last line of your literary productions, or the hour that is to separate them from your Society.

In the name of Misery therefore, I address these pages to you, and, remain,

    Dear Sir,

        Your crabbed Friend,

        F. MURMUR.

TO THE PUBLIC.

I THOUGHT of asking a friend of mine who edited one of the best cookery books in our language to retouch and beautify Sir Fretful Murmur's introductory memoir, and his letters, bas they are intelligible, and moreover as the worthy Knight would not like to appear in patch work, though many of the *pieces were of satin*; I have ventured to lay his effusions before the Public just as I received them from Fen Lodge.

GILES WHIMBLE

CONTENTS.

LETTER I..18
Violent attack of the ague; celebration of Dorothea's fiftieth year; talks of changing her condition.

LETTER II...29
Dorothea's dispute with Mr. Debit; Turkies not lay the same number of eggs in war as in peace; Debit's Terrier, and sister's favourite Fiddy.

LETTER III..36
Exercising Volunteers; great Men of St. Stephen's: Military Blunder.

LETTER IV..45
Silly repetition of a Princess ; Debit's reconciliation.

LETTER V..55
Marriage of Dorothea; pompous procession ; Cats wore bridal favours; Journey to London.

LETTER VI..63
Mr. And Mrs. Debit's excursion to Brighton; Marriage spoils our fine young women ; accomplishments of pickling and preserving ; purchase of baby linen.

CONTENTS.

LETTER VII..73
Mr. and Mrs. D. Going to see Mrs. Siddons; Mr. Debit's silly repetition; confusion of the audience.

LETTER VIII..80
Dorothea's ridiculous behaviour at Brighton; thrown from a Jerusalem Poney; amusement of the spectators; Mr. Debit's escape from drowning.

LETTER IX..86
Dislike to the French; dismissing the Grocer; Frenchmen made like monkeys; Green Man; sea bathing favourable to procreation.

LETTER X..92
Sarah subpoened to attend the quarter sessions; cross examined by Mr Jekyll the Witty Barrister; Sarah's witty reply.

LETTER XI..98
Application of a celebrated Philosopher; Sapient country Magistrate; the Prince's Stables at Brighton; Horses standing on Persian Carpets; the Emerald Gentleman.

LETTER XII..103
Mr. and Mrs. Debit's return to Town; Botanical Lecture in Albermarle Street; disposition of the grass; Eliza giggling.

MEMOIR.

NATURE having made me one of those gossamer, sensitive beings, upon whom the breath of Heaven cannot blow without more or less agitation, I amused myself last year with keeping a Diary of Vexations which I at first called *Recontres Fucheux* [1], till being fretted into a mortal antipathy against the French I changed that title for *Vexatious Trifles* [2], intending to produce them one day or another to prove to the world, by what tiny circumstances, the tranquillity of an irritable man may be disturbed. I moreover found that to describe these teasing troubles was to disarm them of their sting, and that one might as quietly contemplate them afterwards as a fine lady might a mouse in a cage, until she wondered that so diminutive an animal could have annoyed her, and resolved that the scratching and midnight rambles of its kindred should her no more in future.

With all these good and right benevolent intentions in my head and heart, I found myself in part delightfully anticipated by "*The Miseries of Human Life*"; or, "*The Groans of Samuel Sensitive and Timothy Testy, with a few Supplementary Sighs from Mrs. Testy.*" The writer of this whimsical work, has with exquisite power of elucidation delineated many of the disquietudes which I endured, but as some that description and other which my acquaintances have suffered remained untold, I thought with my friend Whimble's assistance, that I could send another little Catalogue of Petty Torments into the world, that the morbid, the melancholy, and the irritable may taste the *peculiar felicity* of having in their possession a *full enumeration* of the various causes of those grievances which force us to go groaning on in our pilgrimage through life, in imitation of some persons who always preserve in cotton the extracted tooth, or in a phial the worm which have tormented them.

This is the first time, I ever appeared in print, but with the terror of battalions of Reviewers before me who suffer nothing however trifling, to escape their keen and ardent eye, I have ventured to present my little volume to the Public in a

---

[1] Facheux: unfortunate, annoying, awkward. Recontre: recount/tell a tale.
[2] And 200 years later ...

dress completely different from that of my able forerunner in the *Valley of Tears*, with my name boldly though not proudly affixed to it.

I have one objection however to the work which I have spoken of which so much admiration, viz. to the numerous Latin quotations with which it abounds, but which I candidly confess arises in no inconsiderable degree from my having forgotten nearly all the Latin which the birch drove into my head, through rather a circuitous passage, when I was at school : in all other respects the *Miseries of Human Life are enviable.*

The troubles of our earthly pilgrimage may be divided into three classes

Imaginary Miseries
Minor Miseries
and
Mighty Miseries

The first are produced by brains sufficiently distempered to cherish such shadowy evils without playing off any other eccentricity : they make the rich man think that want and famine are about to seize him, and the vigorous man that he is the victim of more than half the diseases enumerated in the Family Physician. As these miseries supply the want of substantial affliction they cannot be too forcibly recommended to those who are blessed with so much felicity that they would be puzzled to create a wish which cannot be gratified. Shakespeare whose chequered life allowed him experimentally to characterise this sort of visitation describes it to be

_____ *"False Sorrow's eye
which for things true weeps things imaginary"*

These visionary fiends though viewless as the winds are frequently as mischievous, and aided by a *green metropolitan fog,* and a north-easter in November, are the very best friends that Suicide can call her own.

Under their inspiring influence a female friend of mine in the enjoyment of a pretty, and healthy person, and about two thousand per annum, took to solitary *cabinet bibbing* [3] until mounted upon the curling vapour of cherry brandy and

---

[3] Drinking heartily from the drinks cabinet!

Ratafia, her gentle spirit evaporated into thin air; and a fine dashing fellow whom I have frequently met in society of which he was the soul, at the age of thirty, rich, vigorous, and forever laughing, left upon his table a note addressed to me, declaring that the only reason which had induced him to place the muzzle of a pistol to his head was that he was completely tired of the intolerable repetition of putting his breeches on every day.

In the fashionable world, these evils frequently deaden the lustre of the most brilliant candelabra, whilst those who tread the paths of rural humility are too industrious to be unhealthy, and have not time to be unhappy. However if I possessed the power of expelling those evils, family considerations would induce me to forbear : I have a first cousin who is a fashionable physician in a high practice whose pocket *imaginary evil fills* with *substantial good.*

With respect to *Minor Miseries*, what they want in size they make up in number and variety. We may escape the pressure of gigantic evil, and never feel an imaginary one, but even the Child of Fortune, and an angel in temper cannot elude those *musquito vexations* which just *curl* without agitating our tranquillity, and which like the Lilliputian arrows that in showers, made Gulliver roar with anguish, affect us by quick succession in close column, when singly they are perfectly harmless. Such are the miseries contained in the following pages, amongst which I have interspersed some whimsical facts, not so generally felt.

The huge calamities of life require no illustration – may no reader of mine be ever brushed by the tail of their storm.

This essay, the first I ever wrote, being over, I shall conclude by giving a brief account of myself.

My father and mother, weak as hothouse plants, died in the prime of life of declines, leaving five children (having had eight) of whom I and Dorothea were left the shivering survivors, they dropping off in consumptions, generally preceded by the rupture of blood vessels.

The founders of Rome were nourished by a wolf, and I owed my preservation to the milk of a she ass, which to this hour makes me reverence the long eared race with almost filial affection.

I remember (always having a singular facility or rather genius for weeping,) that upon the death of a brother when I was ten years old, I wept so copiously, that my mother was quite charmed with me, praised me very much for it, and turning round to a sister was one year younger than myself, who was amusing herself with her doll, said "There, Fanny, look at your Brother Fretful, see how he cries, and you have not shed one tear." Upon which I roared more bitterly, and received a large piece of plumb cake, for the drops I shed open the occasion.

We had a cross French valet, who at the age of fourteen taught the following Song,

>Chacun se fair des plaisirs a sa mode,
>   Et selon son temperament:
>Pourmoi, qui suis chagrin, et que tout incommode
>   Je prens mon divertissment,
>   A gronder tant que le jour dure
>   Sans pouvoir, je le jure,
>   M'imaginer comment,
>   Aucun se peut diverir autrument.

>It is in the mind's peculiar hue,
>   That tints the pleasure we pursue,
>To sad chagrin a prey,
>   I find supreme delight
>   In scolding, and in spite,
>   And from my soul I cannot tell
>   How time can e'er be pass'd so well,
>   In any other way.

At twenty I went upon the continent, where I found abundant sources for discontent in bad inns, bad roads, carriages without springs, and meat done to rags. Upon my return to England I took chambers in the Temple, where my spleen only increased - everything fidgeted me ; in my time, it was the rage to give fine names to common children, and I remember quitting a coffee-house in disgust, because I overhead the Host exclaim:
"Anna Maria, don't you hear the pot is boiling over."

Then there was the pomp and folly of funerals. Although the wife of a butcher abhorred her husband mortally, yet the moment the breath was out of his body, "the poor dear soul must have a handsome funeral, a velvet pall, with brass handles and hinges to the coffin, tombstone and a *Latin* epitaph." Then the rage for virtue and enormous sums paid for monsters of every denomination, dried, stuffed, and floating in spirits, then the public nuisances of the metropolis, carts delivering or taking in loads in narrow streets, and ladies cultivating the science of botany by means of pots set on the leads two or three stories high, which in windy weather were frequently blown down, then to see tradesmen in the City clumsily imitating their superiors at the west end of the town, then the number of beggars swarming in the streets with borrowed or stolen children, with a long etcetera, which soon drove me to my old family mansion, which I determined to reside in wholly for the future, bet here a thousand vexations pursued me, for here the neighbouring fens frequently produced the ague, and Dorothea growing old and cross because she grew old, worried me to fiddle strings, for she never ceased scolding the maids but when she was collecting eggs, feeding the turkies, or assisting at the lying-ins, that happened in the parish.

In time I gained a little strength, sufficient to fill, which I did with infinite disgust, the magisterial chair of our corporation, and upon presenting a congratulatory address to the throne, received the honour of a knighthood. Since which time, I have rarely moved to encounter something to wound my over sensitive feelings.

If however my irritable reader derives the same comfort from the perusal of my Supplemental Miseries, as I have done from the Miseries of Human Life, then *will these sheets be like flowers in the chamber of sickness that inhale the unwholesome air and breath it out again with refreshing purity.*

F. MURMUR

Fen Lodge, 1st November 1806

MORE MISERIES, &c.

MORE MISERIES, &c.

LETTER I.

Fen-Lodge.

MY DEAR WHIMBLE,

YOU should have received my first Budget of MORE MISERIES earlier, but for a violent attack of the Ague. As often as I thought myself a little better, and sat up to copy them from my memory, a shivering fit came on, and shook the pen out of my hand.

I am now, thank Heaven and the Doctor out again. My sister Dorothea sends her compliments – we celebrated her fiftieth year yesterday ; she talks of speedily changing her condition. I shall not be sorry for it, for between ourselves, *she is not a misery to laugh at.*

YOURS EVER,

F. MURMUR

MISERIES.

I.1 Sitting to have your teeth filed.

I.2 Residing between a Stone-cutter's and an Undertaker's.

I.3 Wearing false tops to your half-boots and observing that one of them has slided down, just as a party of dashing women are passing by.

I.4 Being obliged to press very hard, a very damp, or what is called a *puggy* hand.

I.5 After a violent attack of the ague, assisting a very short fat lady over a very high stile, the steps having been that morning stolen.

I.6 Being obliged to hear a very dull proser relate a very long story, principally relating to himself and his own family.

The following misery I well remember occurring to a very particular and very vain friend of mine – its whimsicality will be an apology for its length.

I.7 Sending to the Morning Post, a paragraph written by *yourself*, announcing the arrival of yourself and family in town, in the following words; "Yesterday Mr. and the charming Mrs. F. And their *three lovely* and *accomplished* daughters arrived at their townhouse in Burlington Street from Moss Hall in Kent, which beautiful retreat, has undergone some alterations from the exquisite designs of Mrs. F. whose unrivalled taste is the theme of admiration amongst all her numerous fashionable friends and acquaintance." Meeting three days after the appearance of the paragraph an acquaintance, who informs you to your great gratification that he had read the arrival : then upon your modestly observing thereon, that "it is a singular thing that one cannot move without being watching by these confounded Newspaper writers, and that it is really wonderful how they can get the intelligence they publish." Your friend laughing in your face, and telling you that he was in the Newspaper Office to get a puff for a friend of his inserted at the time, when your servant came in with and paid for the paragraph you mentioned, which lying on the counter he perused and recognised to be in *your own hand-writing*.

I.8 Being requested by a foreigner who understands very little of the English language, to hear him read Milton.

I.9 In consequence of losing all your money at cards in the evening, having none to give the servants the next morning, when you are quitting a house, where you are not very intimate, reconciling yourself to the shabbiness of the dilemma by feeling satisfied, that you shall never enter the doors again ; being obliged on account of particular business to visit it a fortnight afterwards, and finding that the only attention the servants pay you, is to throw some soup accidentally over your best coat.

I.10 Haggling with a surly hackney-coachman for sixpence, and after he has driven off about a quarter-of-an-hour, recollecting that you have left a new umbrella in his coach.

I.11 Giving a commission to a painter and leaving it to him to choose the subject and when the picture is sent home, wishing that he had selected any other, than that chosen.

I.12 All your acquaintance telling you, that a portrait which you are aware is *rather flattering*, is not at all like you.

I.13 Ordering a tumbler of warm brandy and water at an inn, upon putting your lips to it, finding it boiling hot, the coachman swearing that he can stay only one minute longer, after blowing the surface a hundred times, almost consuming your inside by the boiling draught -- all this to prevent being sick.

I.14 Diffidently entering a full room, every chair occupied, and no one standing to keep you company.

I.14 : Diffidently entering a full room, every chair occupied, and no one standing to keep you company.

I.15 *A friend of mine a young Barrister experienced the following misery*

> Not having paid your devotions very ardently to Coke upon Littleton and particularly having neglected "the whole law relative to the duty and office of a justice of the peace," being asked at dinner before a large party, by a country magistrate, your opinion upon a plain settlement point, which has bewildered him ; giving a wrong one, and confounded by being, in a knowing and officious manner, set right by a rip of a petty-fogging country attorney ; who was honoured by an invitation at the same table.

I.16 Expecting a remittance, and receiving a stupid set of anonymous verses by the post.

I.17 Upon your return to England, receiving per post a long letter, written to you whilst on the continent by your servant, informing you who called, &c. Which arriving after you had quitted the place to which it was directed, is forwarded to you in a fresh cover, a week after your return, and for which you pay a monstrous postage.

I.18 Writing upon a thin sheet of paper, very small crumbs of bread under it.

I.19 Dropping and leaving the address of a fair frail friend in the room of the lady to whom you are paying your addresses.

I.20 Calling on a sultry day upon a friend who has the mania for planting upon him ; who after marching and counter-marching you three or four miles to see his plantations, irresistibly presses you to ascend a considerable eminence of ground, about half a mile off, to see a couple of Weymouth pines which he planted on the day when his first child was born.

I.21 When a boy, scratching and staining your hands in endeavouring to get blackberries out of reach.

I.22 On a sultry day, putting your hand into your breeches pocket, in withdrawing the former, turning the latter inside out, and seeing a guinea roll to and vanish through a chink in the floor.

I.23 At breakfast, honey dropping through the apertures of your bread, and over the sides, upon your fingers, before you have half covered the surface.

I.24 Upon the continent having a companion who does not understand a word of the language spoken, every moment asking you to translate what any foreigner may be saying to you, before he has finished.

I.25 Shooting London Bridge with weak nerves, several ladies of the party.

I.26 Going to dine, rather behind your time in a new coat, passing under a lamp-iron whilst a lamplighter is trimming a lamp, and being lubricated by a considerable portion of his filthy oil.

I.27 Singing at a tavern, being frequently interrupted by a waiter entering, and exciting considerable indignation, by so doing in the company, also by the clock striking the *longest hour*, ditto by one of the part (having no ear for music,) cracking a walnut, &c. &c.

I.28 Explaining to your servant, who is anything but a mechanic, how easy it is to set a steel rat-trap, and just as you have said to him, "There, now, you see the least thing in the world will set it off!" you prove to him the truth of your assertion, by its unexpectedly embracing your own thumb.

I.29 Drying a long letter by the fire, holding it negligently in one hand behind you whilst you are conversing with a friend in the room, turning round and perceiving it to be in flames.

I.30 Being persecuted by a female beggar along several streets, and in spite of a determination to give her nothing, being obliged to give her sixpence, having no halfpence, to get rid of her.

I.28 : Explaining to your servant, who is anything but a mechanic, how easy it is to set a steel rat-trap, and just as you have said to him, "There, now, you see the least thing in the world will set it off!" you prove to him the truth of your assertion, by its unexpectedly embracing your own thumb.

I.31 Reading a very interesting book by a small green wax taper, which is in want of constant elevation.

I.32 Sitting opposite to a man who squints, and answering him when he is addressing another person.

I.33 Hearing the monotonous scream of parish boys and girls, singing an anthem.

I.34 Carelessly stooping to blow your nose, coming in contact with a porter, carrying a high and heavy box on his knot, as you rise and recede, tilting said box over.

I.35 Attending three country cousins to the Opera, who after staring about them as if they had just come out of a convent, constantly and audibly ask you, who such and such a person is with a star, at the same time, to prevent all possibility of your mistaking the object, directing their finger towards him.

I.36 Hearing a lovely young woman, whose good opinion you wish to conciliate, speak in raptures of a trinket which she has seen at a jeweller's, purchasing it for an exorbitant price, presenting it to her in an awkward way and being mortified by a polite but firm refusal.

I.37 Having a pimple on your chin, covering it with sticking plaster, and just as you enter the drawing room, discovering that it curls on all sides.

I.38 Walking down a very long street, with a head-ache, in the wake of a dustman's cart, the dustman constantly announcing his approach by the clapper of a singularly shrill bell.

I.39 After sporting with a most enchanting creature's fan just before the close of a ball, putting it in your pocket, meaning to keep it as a little trophy ; receiving a message from her the next morning by her maid servant requesting you will return it.

I.40 Being prevailed upon by your friend to accompany him to a dinner party to which you have not been invited, and upon your introduction to the lady of the house, she expresses her regret that her dining room is so small and immediately afterwards obliquely observes with a freezing but , that she can manage very well, as her brother can sit at a side table.

I.41   Being bored by a man whom you do not like, to dine with him, and being nailed by his begging you to fix your own day.

I.42   After the battle of Helder or Seringapatam, at which you were not present, walking up and down Bond Street with your *sound arm in a sling*, overhearing that you are smoked by some dashing fashionables, as they pass you.

I.43   Being invited to a wedding dinner, when you have just discovered the inconstancy of your wife.

I.44   Having a boy trundle his hoop against your legs, in which you get entangled, said hoop having divers and sundry bits of musical tin fastened to it — clean silk stockings —

———>•◆•<———

I.44 : Having a boy trundle his hoop against your legs, in which you get entangled, said hoop having divers and sundry bits of musical tin fastened to it — clean silk stockings —

DOROTHEA, is still single, and I in consequence still very uncomfortable.

LETTER II.

Fen-Lodge.

MY DEAR WHIMBLE,

DOROTHEA, is still single, and I in consequence still very uncomfortable. She has had a violent dispute with Mr. Debit, a gentleman well known at the Stock Exchange, to whom she was betrothed, in consequence of his asserting that war to us, as a commercial state, was a national blessing, she maintaining on the contrary, that it was so extensive an evil, that she could prove by her diary, that even turkies do not lay the same number of eggs in war as they do in times of political amity.

Mr. Debit has set out for London in a tiff, no doubt, thinking that although war is unquestionably very delightful *abroad*, it is far otherwise at *home*. What I believe has more violently fermented the quarrel is, that in the midst of the argument, Pincher, Mr. Debit's terrier, bit sister's favourite Fiddy, whose breath used to annoy you so, of which bite she died this morning. All these vexations, and the increasing fidgets of Dorothea, are the reasons for my not having sent you MORE MISERIES on the third day after I received your esteemed favour.

YOURS EVER,

F. MURMUR

MORE MISERIES.

II.1 In sharply turning a corner, coming suddenly in contact with a chimney-sweeper, who impresses your white waistcoat and light coloured breeches with very visible memorials of the *rencontre* [3].

II.2 Passing in London under a gallipot garden [4], which you had not observed, projecting from a window, just at the moment when its rural mistress is watering her half withered swarthy sweet peas and myrtles, the mould hard, and the water running over into the street.

II.3 When a boy — being asked if you will have any more mince pie, blushingly saying no, and immediately afterwards wishing the mortifying negative at the devil.

II.4 During a fracas in the street, between two blackguards, praising the superior prowess and skill of one of them in the hearing of a man who is the friend of the party at whose expense this compliment is paid, and who begins to defend his friend in such language, and with such gesticulations, that you deem it most advisable to retreat, with infinite caution and address, from the scene of action.

II.5 A very thin house in Drury Lane.

II.6 Living in chambers under a man who takes private lessons in dancing.

II.7 Receiving a bountiful splash upon your face and neck cloth, from a wheel of a heavily laden cart, suddenly dropping into a puddle of mud water in a narrow street, and being followed by an audacious little butcher's boy, who constantly keeps a little before you, every now and then looking up and grinning in your face.

II.8 Finding a man growing warm with you on some very private and delicate family topic in a coffee-room, where you observe everyone is listening and smiling.

---

[3] A word no longer used in French – n. Meeting or an encounter.
[4] A ceramic plant pot used for growing medicinal herbs.

II.9 As you are walking with two ladies, being followed by a drunken sailor and his trull[5], both talking very loudly and indecently, your endeavours by a quick step and rapid observation, to prevent the ladies from hearing.

II.10 Passing Millbank at low water with a party of ladies, between groups of bathers, some in the water, and some standing or sitting upon floats of timber.

II.11 Condemned to sit in a room where a piano forte is tuning.

II.12 Sitting at dinner next to a man of consequence with whom you wish to ingratiate yourself, being told that he has superstitious horror at the salt being spilt, and from excess of caution sending the contents of the salt cellar into his plate.

II.13 Walking arm in arm with a man of fashion to whom you have been recently introduced, and meeting a vulgar acquaintance.

II.14 Quitting your friend's arm for a moment, who walks on whilst you speak a few words on a very important subject to a person whom you meet, upon leaving him seizing the arm of a stranger for that of your friend.

II.15 When in the act of eating with an excellent appetite, or in the middle of a very interesting conversation, having your health drank and pertinaciously repeated until you are made to hear and thank your tormentor.

II.16 Seeing a cow skip and frisk, and affect the graces.

II.17 Passing over a brown bladeless common.

II.18 To be obliged to listen to a sharp savage old maid, whilst she relates the scandal of the village, you not being acquainted with any creature in it, except the narratrix.

---

[5] A prostitute, commonly associated with sailors.

II.12: Sitting at dinner next to a man of consequence with whom you wish to ingratiate yourself, being told that he has superstitious horror at the salt being spilt, and from excess of caution sending the contents of the salt cellar into his plate.

II.19 Returning from a rural walk, being obliged to go through a lane, under the lee of heaps of burning weeds.

II.20 Passing a narrow passage fresh painted.

II.21 Forced by politeness to quit a comfortable party to attend a cross old maid to her lodgings at the distance of two miles.

II.22 Putting coals on fire, the handle of a coal-scuttle being dirty — new gloves on.

II.23 The sensations of a crabbed, disappointed, hatchet-faced, skinnylipped spinster, hovering upon the frontier of despair upon seeing a group of blooming, lovely and elegant young women enter the room.

II.24 Whilst you are making a sketch, having a number of impertinent persons staring behind you, until the crowd increases to that degree, that you are obliged to abandon your subject.

II.25 Wishing to wake early to be in time for a morning coach, waking and upon looking at your watch discovering that you had not wound it up.

II.26 Being interrogated by an irritable author respecting a quarto work, a copy of which he presented you six months before, and by your answers satisfying him, though you wish to conceal it, that you have not read one word of it.

II.27 Attending private theatricals, where the gentlemen performers always press near the prompter's side, always hurry over passages in order to catch every word before it slips from the memory, one performer not giving the cue word, or giving it, not remembered by the other who plays with him, standing like posts when they have nothing to say, and when moving using their legs and arms as if they had been just bestowed upon them.

II.28   In chambers, having only one room with a fire place, the throat of the chimney perpetually disgorging large volumes of smoke, the blacks falling about you as thick as snow, until your eyes are sore, opening the doors and windows and perishing with cold in front of an immense fire — a large party to dine with you and one of them much affected with an asthma.

II.29   Asking a lady to permit you to look at a beautiful string of very small pearls, breaking it in two, scattering them over the floor, and crushing several under your feet in endeavouring to collect them.

II.30   Moistening the only wafer in the house so long in your mouth, that upon taking it out you find it like a bit of rotten pear.

II.31   In endeavouring to fold a letter up very neatly, splitting the corners with your ivory knife.

II.32   Striking your foot against another step after you had concluded that you had reached the top of the stairs.

II.33   Upon a journey, having made some important memorandums in your pocket book, with a soft pencil, and finding every letter rendered illegible — memory bad.

II.34   Breaking your spectacles a considerable distance from any town.

II.35   Arriving in the winter, at the Gloucester Coffee-House in the western mail at six o'clock of a cold drizzly morning, and finding the only servant up engaged in scouring the back parlour, into which you are shown.

II.36   Being asked to dine with an author and after dinner his pulling out a long manuscript and reading until you must inevitably fall asleep, were you not constantly kept on the *qui vive*, by his asking you how you like this passage, and how that.

II.29 : Asking a lady to permit you to look at a beautiful string of very small pearls, breaking it in two, scattering them over the floor, and crushing several under your feet in endeavouring to collect them.

LETTER III.

Fen-Lodge.

I am glad to find by your letter, my dear Whimble, that you like my miseries. Vexations *described*, and vexations *felt* are very different, so much so, that I can now even laugh whilst I portray many of those grievances, which I endured, and without a smile, I assure you. In addition to the miseries which I send you, as I know you like whimsical things, laugh if you like at the following anecdote which occurred yesterday in, exercising our volunteers ; by the bye, I ought to preface it by observing, that I admire the volunteer system, as much as any man, though in my poor opinion, your great men at St. Stephen's made a sad blunder in permitting a volunteer to hold any rank *but* in his own particular description of service. Now for the anecdote — In the absence of the Captain of our volunteers, the Lieutenant, a respectable farmer, had the command of the company ; this worthy Officer, wanting to halt his men, who were marching in a most irregular manner, could not recollect the word "halt," in this dilemma he cried out, "Wooee, wooee, woo, wooee, my boys" when the whole body immediately halted. Dorothea seems more composed : she has no yet heard from Mr. Debit, but if I know anything of human nature she speedily will,

Ever yours,

F. MURMUR.

MORE MISERIES.

III.1 Toasting a bit of bread at the end of a short dessert fork, before a good brisk fire, and burning the ends of your fingers without being able to toast it to your liking.

III.2 Being surrounded by a parcel of spoiled, squalling brats, 'till you are almost induced to think favourably of Herod.

III.3 Attending ladies on a shopping excursion.

III.4 Stepping out of a boat at low water in pumps, well-dressed, upon a stone which slides under you and you descend ankle deep in mud.

III.5 Rubbing the back of your hand by mistake against the liquefying gum of a plumb-tree.

III.6 At a game at forfeits[6] saluting a pretty-looking girl, and finding that her teeth are not of aromatic pearl.

III.7 A fine overture playing, and a noisy audience.

III.8 The miseries, in the shape of mistakes, which two persons of the same name, residing within four doors of each other, experience.

III.9 In a cold night, long legs and a short camp bed.

III.10 In frosty weather descending a piece of ground here and there covered with thin hard ice, slipping down, in falling laying hold of the ankle of a prudish elderly spinster with who you are walking, and drawing her after you.

III.11 A female pun.

III.12 Sleeping over your wine, gradually driving your glass to the edge of the table, and then, by another somnolent movement, throwing it over a new pair of leathers.

---

[6] Forfeits. A parlour game for anything up to 25 players or more.

iii.9 : In a cold night, long legs and a short camp bed.

III.13   Wearing flannel drawers and waistcoat for the first time.

III.14   Climbing a cherry tree to gratify a young lady, and splitting your small clothes, just as you are gracefully stretching to drop two beautiful white hearts in her handkerchief, which she holds below.

III.15   Having succeeded in fixing yourself in a most seducing and graceful attitude, letting your cocked hat fall.

III.16   Making several memorandum knots in your handkerchief, and forgetting the important cause of every one of them.

III.17   Knocking at a door, and by a horrible and unaccountable lapse of memory forgetting the name of the master or mistress of the house.

III.18   Having made a trip to Paris, during the short peace, being bored to death by every soul you meet with, to describe Bonaparte.

III.19   A collector of natural curiosities worrying you with a description of his invaluable tortoiseshell boar cat, his kitten with three eyes, his pig with with one ear, &c. &c.

III.20   Being conducted by an enthusiastic agriculturalist round an extensive farm, having no taste whatever for the breeding of sheep, fattening of pigs, new invented draining and threshing machines, &c. &c.

III.21   Being seized with a violent bowel complaint, whilst you are riding on horseback with two young ladies, to one of whom you are paying your addresses, being obliged to sit alight in great confusion, telling your fair companions, that there is an exquisite bit of scenery around a hedge, which you have just passed, and which you should like very much to sketch, assuring them that you will return in five minutes, and remembering afterwards that it was well known you never drew in your life.

III.22   Being required by a garrulous old lady, to know where she left off in a long story, which she was relating to you, she having been interrupted in the middle of it by the servant delivering a message to her, not being able to inform her, in consequence of not having attended to one word that she had been saying.

III.23 Hearing that a young lady to whom you are ardently attached, and who you flattered yourself regarded you favourably, is displaying uncommon vivacity and spirits, at a distant watering place, and that she is everywhere much admired.

III.24 In the Volunteers — being short and fat, cased in fleecy hosiery, at the instance of your fond wife, to guard against the effect of sudden showers, having the command of a small attacking party of light infantry at a sham fight, and encountering stiles, gates, hedges and at least ten thousand sharp stubs and stumps in the course of your evolutions — day very sultry.

III.25 Passing with a shy horse in a gig in a narrow part of the Strand, the Paviors[7] repairing a broken water pipe on one side of you, and a long heavily laden coal cart approaching you on the other, the driver talking to a friend a little way behind in this dilemma affecting to look cool and collected with dismay in your soul, and the perspiration starting from every pore.

III.26 Having just composed yourself to take a nap on your sofa, eternally tormented by two flies, in the middle of October whom you could almost swear to, but cannot catch, and who judiciously prefer alighting and washing their hands and faces on your nose and forehead, to regaling on an adjoining saucer full of sweet poison.

III.27 After keeping within doors three days, from horrible nervous dislike to an east wind, which by the weathercock fronting your chamber, appeared to have been blowing during that period, to be told by a wag that he had fastened the vane due east, whilst it had been blowing due west all the time.

---

[7] The Paviors are 56th in order of preference of the City Livery Companies. They were granted Royal Charter in 2004. Their main tasks at the time were public ordinances.

III.28   Shooting Chelsea Bridge in a sailing boat, and not lowering the mast in time, which is broken by the rencontre, the vessel lying like a log in the water, yourself exposed to the length of spectators on the bridge above, and the criticising derision of the watermen below.

III.29   Tempted by a fine summer evening to take an *easy row* on the water, and on your endeavours to display your skill in feathering your oar, as a party passes by losing one of your sculls, which being lighter, goes faster than the boat and being perplexed by a mob of modes pointed out by the persons who observe your distress for recovering of said scull.

III.30   Entering upon any of the bridges of London, or any of the passages leading to the Thames, being assailed by a group of watermen, holding up their hands and bawling out, "Oars, Sir, Sculls, Sir, Sculls, Sir, Oars, Sir."

III.31   Upon paying the first visit after the funeral of a relation, a distant cousin for instance, to the immediate friends of the deceased, finding them all in tears and from some unaccountable counteraction of nature, not being able to look grave upon the occasion.

III.32   Having so flaccid a cheek that the parish barber who shaves you, is obliged to introduce his thumbs into your mouth to give it a proper projection; cutting his thumb in this position, with the razor.

III.33   Dreaming that you have wings and waking with a fit of the gout.

III.34   Handing round, when a child, a plate of plumb cake, and seeing the last bit left, on which you had fixed your eye and heart, taken by one of the party.

III.35   To be the child of a wet nurse, and sent to share with another infant, a nipple strongly impregnated with Geneva, Sky-Blue and other nutritious liquors.

iii.33: Dreaming that you have wings and waking with a fit of the gout.

III.36   Going to the Theatre on a very crowded night, waiting an hour in the pit passage half jammed to death, receiving a dreadful kick on the ankle in making a desperate effort to stoop down to rub it, finding your hand in the coat pocket of the man who stands opposite to you, and gradually withdrawing it with indescribable horror, so as just to escape being taken up for a pick-pocket.

III.37   Sleeping in a dark room, in a dark night, in a strange house, and after being kept awake by the most mysterious sounds for three hours, at length, beginning to be satisfied that they proceed from an unusually active mouse.

III.38   A long dead calm at sea in a Dutch galleon, during a short passage, bad accommodations and provisions nearly exhausted.

III.39   Being tormented by a flea, which, during a visit crawling up your leg under the boot, so that your fingers can administer no relief.

III.40   In a party being suddenly overwhelmed with a disposition to sleep, nodding every now and then, and giving an answer to a question put by a person who does not perceive that you are between sleeping and waking which you fear may have no connection with the question.

III.41   Ditto ineffectually rousing yourself and endeavouring by random comments upon those shattered portions of the conversation which you have heard, to make it appear that you have been as attentive as the rest of the party.

III.42   A favourite dog in the mange.

III.43   Travelling in a mail-coach one hundred and eighty miles, and all the way having your nose offended by the most horrible stench which each of the passengers thinks proceeds from his neighbour, and upon arriving at the Swan with Two Necks, Lad-Lane, discovering that the *mauvaise odeur* issued from a putrid hare in one of the seats, which owing to the carelessness of the guard has been permitted to perform two journeys to town.

The Swan with Two Necks, Lad-Lane was built around 1630 and had closed by 1867. Lad Lane became Gresham Street and can be found in Cheapside, London.

LETTER IV.

Fen-Lodge.

DEAR WHIMBLE,

YOU made me smile at the account of your interview with Lord D____. His Lordship is certainly not one of the wise men of the east ; his repetition of his silly question which you had previously answered, reminds me of the story of a princess who asked a lady who was presented to her, how many children she had, to which she replied, three ; about a quarter of an hour afterward, the princess met her again, and not knowing what to say, put the same question to her, to which she answered "that not having lain in since her highness had asked her the same question she had *still* only three children."

Debit has made the first advances to a reconciliation, so I hope all things will go on smoothly, notwithstanding the war. I have the happiness of sending you some more miseries, and remain,

Ever yours,

F. MURMUR.

MORE MISERIES.

IV.1 Having lost your way being in great haste and asking a stuttering family to direct you to the place of your destination.

IV.2 The wife of a clerk in a public office at a low salary, producing twins once a year.

IV.3 Being asked by an absent man to dinner, and upon your arriving at his house finding him just set off for the country.

IV.4 A melancholy man dying of the hip seeing a hearse draw up and stop before his door. —P.S. The coachman gone to the public house, so that there is no possibility of removing it.

IV.5 In repeating some verses with uncommon animation and emphases, to a party on the water, tipping over the side of the boat, and being taken up, after a most mortifying ducking.

IV.6 Hearing ladies talk politics.

IV.7 Having a long back and discovering that the irons which fasten the back of the seat in a boat are disordered and useless.

IV.8 Having your portrait finely painted in crayons, spoiled by your favourite Newfoundland dog, who struck with the resemblance, begins licking it, whilst the servant is cleaning the glass and frame.

IV.9 Crossing a yard, and unexpectedly finding yourself within the extent of the chain of a large surly house-dog, affecting boldly to look him in the face, and in an agony of horror, gradually stealing away from him.

IV.10 Being squeezed in a crowd, and having a little dwarf with red hair, jammed up against you, immediately under your nose.

IV.11 Trying to pass a man who waddles.

IV.8 : Having your portrait finely painted in crayons, spoiled by your favourite Newfoundland dog, who struck with the resemblance, begins licking it, whilst the servant is cleaning the glass and frame.

IV.12 Soon after you have comfortably seated yourself in the drawing room of a fashionable family in the country, where you are to sleep for the night, having your comb and night-cap taken out of your pocket and laid on the floor, by a pert, spoiled, impudent child, and find the room in a titter at your expense.

IV.13 Nineteen prologues out of twenty.

IV.14 Being obliged to attend a very *absent* man to a party of prudish ladies, and being fearful that every moment he will bolt out or do something highly indecorous.

IV.15 Having a refusal to an offer of marriage sent by an inquisitive maid servant, before the *wafer is dry*.

IV.16 Opening and shutting a drawer which has swelled by the damp.

IV.17 Being obliged to hear a stupid fellow boggle at a speech after dinner, upon being informed that his health has been drank, during his absence from the room.

IV.18 Receiving an insipid answer to a letter from a very absent man, who in his forgetfulness has folded up four sheets of paper instead of one, and for which you have the happiness of paying a heavy additional postage.

IV.19 Hastily saluting a lady, and afterwards discovering she has an *unroselike* breath.

IV.20 Adjusting long unsettled accounts with a peevish partner, or an ignorant and suspicious tradesman.

IV.21 Endeavouring to make violent love under the table, and pressing the wrong foot.

IV.22 Plunging for a rhyme to a good line and after many desperate efforts, being obliged to tag another which either contains the same sentiments.

IV.10 : Being squeezed in a crowd, and having a little dwarf with red hair, jammed up against you, immediately under your nose.

IV.22   Hearing an ode of your own composition, which you think pregnant with Pindaric fire and sublimity called "pretty".

IV.23   Sending your hunter over night to cover, twenty miles off, riding your hack and to the anxious enquiry as to the state of the former's condition, yonr groom informs you that his is *dead lame.*

IV.24   Being prevented from enjoying a day's shooting, by unfortunately tumbling into a wet ditch, covering yourself with mud and filling your gun with water.

IV.25   Finding yourself sleepy, and being requested by the lady of the house, your particular friend, with whom you may make free, to take a nap : having comfortably composed yourself on a sofa, a waggish visitor with whom you are not sufficiently acquainted to authorize such a liberty, but whom you have seen too often to quarrel with on account of it, amusing himself and the party present, by tickling your nostrils with a piece of paper rolled up to a point, awaking hoping that he will not repeat it, sleeping again and finding the torment repeated.

IV.26   Dining with an avaricious fellow who has no idea of the comforts of a cheerful glass and conversation after dinner, or is unwilling to encourage them, being asked by him whether you will take a glass of wine or a walk.

IV.27   At a coffee house, changing the newspaper of the day with a gentleman, that you have read about one third through, for one which you think is a new one, and finding it the paper of yesterday.

IV.28   Being obliged to surrender to a newspaper which you have just begun to read, to another, whose prerogative to the first perusal of it you cannot dispute.

IV.29   Expecting to read great news, receiving your newspaper quite wet from the press, the fire being just lighted.

IV.11 : Trying to pass a man who waddles.

IV.30 In the midst of a merry story being suddenly forced to weep by the sudden operation of an excessive portion of patent and potent mustard.

IV.31 A door slowly turning upon a creaking hinge.

IV.32 Opening a very stiff box filled with small wafers, and spilling them all over the room.

IV.33 Sitting down in the dusk in a chair much shorter than you expected it to be.

IV.34 In attempting to quit a house in London on a Saturday evening, breaking your shins against a pail, and receiving the pole of a mop in your mouth.

IV.35 Swallowing a piece of crust *the wrong way* — several ladies present.

IV.36 Sitting down to dinner with a three pronged fork, each prong being of a different length.

IV.33 : Sitting down in the dusk in a chair much shorter than you expected it to be.

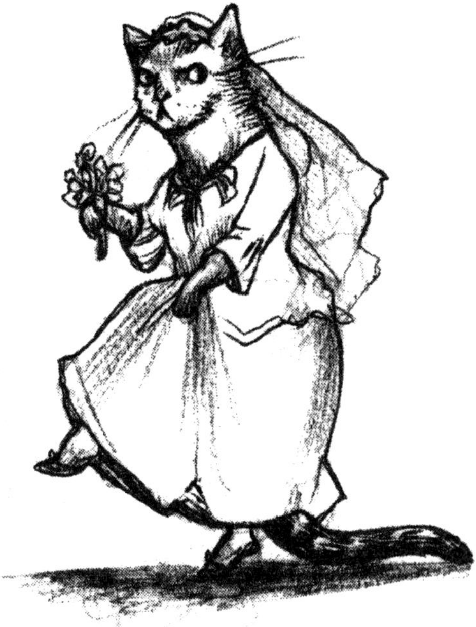

LETTER V.

Fen-Lodge.

CONGRATULATE me, my dear Whimble! Dorothea is at length Mrs. Debit. I, who mortally detest all pomp and show, was obliged to attend *en gala*, to give away the bride, who was preceded by six poor little girls, who are clothed and educated at her expense, strewing flowers before her all the way. She was attired in the Brussels lace and jewels of our worthy mother and grandmother, wore a wreath of jessamine round her head, and looked like the *Dowager Goddess* of May. Her silly appearance really made me splenetic – What a day we had! – I thought I should have gone distracted with the jangling of our two old crazy bells, the third having been sold ten years since to enable the parish to purchase a clock – All was noise and confusion – Even the cats wore bridal favours. Heavens! Be praised, the happy pair are gone to your noisy city, and leave me in tranquillity sufficient to send you a few more delectable miseries.

Ever yours,

F. MURMUR.

MORE MISERIES.

V.1 Being over-persuaded to stand up in a country dance, when you know, or what is equally bad, conceive that a bear would eclipse you in grace and agility.

V.2 Relating a story to a fellow whose apprehension is so slow, that in the middle of a melancholy story, he begins laughing at a merry one which you told him half an hour before.

V.3 Being awaked out of a sound sleep in the dead of a cold, frosty, blowing night, in a mail coach, on the weather wise, by the agreeable address of "Sir, please to remember the guard, I go no further with you, Sir."

V.4 Relating a story very much to the credit of the hero of the piece, when a person very drily observes, that if it had not been for the name, he should have suspected that you were the very person, all the company showing (and with great justice) that they so too.

V.5 Mis-directing your letter to a man whom you have quizzed in it most confoundedly.

V.6 Riding in a full coach twenty miles to dinner, for want of which you are faint and exhausted, wishing to lean back, but not daring to do so, on account of the back of the seat being begrimed with clots of powder and pomatum[8], you wearing no powder.

V.7 Sending a challenge, requesting a timid friend to attend you to the field, who you think will not fail to acquaint the magistrate of it ; going with horror the appointed spot, anxiously looking round every step to see if the Bow-street officers are approaching, without seeing a soul but your antagonist and the seconds.

---

[8] A perfumed hair oil.

V.8   Hastening in the gout to an election which it is supposed will last only a short time, the wheel of your carriage damaged so that you cannot proceed, at a great distance from any wheelwright.

V.9   Toasting a bit of cheese, and when it is more than half done, letting it fall into the ashes.

V.10   Going to the Theatre to see some distinguished play and performer, having places kept ; but owing to some of the party not being ready in time, entering your box just as the first act is over, and observing the last bustle of a number of persons who have just descended into your front seats, and are smirking and smiling to think themselves so very fortunate.

V.11   Carving for a large party with a blunt carving knife.

V.12   Being the first subject which a raw young surgeon's apprentice is permitted to try his professional skill and knowledge upon.

V.13   Having a bill sent in, which you thought you had long since paid.

V.14   Being shaved on the Cornish coast, in the pilchard season, by the parish barber, who embraces your nose with a thumb and finger stinking of said fish.

V.15   At school having pilfered a duck for supper, discovered by the half strangled bird quacking in your pocket, just as one of the masters passes by, and upon being taken up to be flogged hearing two or three purloined eggs fall from your breeches pocket after the first stroke of the rod.

V.16   Walking in a dark night, without lamp, or lantern, upon unequal ground.

V.17   Being requested to say something to entertain the party.

V.18   Compelled by politeness when you are upon a visit at a house, to dance two dances with each of half a dozen ladies belonging to it, at the assize ball, all of whom are either ugly, lame or insipid, and having no opportunity all the evening of going down one dance with a lovely young to whom you are a tenderly attached.

V.14 : Being shaved on the Cornish coast, in the pilchard season, by the parish barber, who embraces your nose with a thumb and finger stinking of said fish.

V.19 Sitting for your portrait to a subordinate painter who renders the likeness with such exasperating exactness that every pimple, blotch and blemish in the face are faithfully represented.

V.20 Having long supporters and sitting opposite to a prudish old maid in a mail coach on a long journey who refuses to open her legs to admit yours which are tingling in every toe with the agony of compression.

V.21 Being invited to meet a party of literary men from who you expect much pleasure, upon your arrival finding them all at cards, and the only person unoccupied, a boisterous gentleman, who can talk of nothing but hounds and horses and thinks he shows his good breeding by perpetually talking to you.

V.22 Being incessantly pestered to eat more, after you have made a hearty dinner.

V.23 In the country, going to a party to dinner, getting very tipsy, quitting the house in a dark night and getting upon your horse with your face towards the tail and wondering during the few minutes that you are able to keep your seat, amongst the jeers of your companions, what freak can have entered the brain of the beast to go backwards.

V.24 Sleeping at an inn, giving your *right* and *left-legged* boots to be cleaned and when you are awaked in the morning and told that the mail is just setting off, calling for your boots and having two left-legged boots brought up, swearing until you glow, at that distinguished personage called Boots, who after a long search is unable to find the right boot, and in consequence, being obliged to hop into the coach with one left boot, and a filthy slipper on, and another left boot in your hand.

V.25 Ditto the equally unpleasant situation of a person to whom the strange boot you carry away belongs, who after you are gone, finds himself in the possession of two boots, which will only fit his right leg.

V23: In the country, going to a party to dinner, getting very tipsy, quitting the house in a dark night and getting upon your horse with your face towards the tail and wondering during the few minutes that you are able to keep your seat, amongst the jeers of your companions, what freak can have entered the brain of the beast to go backwards.

You may remember my telling the following story when I returned from France – it happened to my companion, and I dare say has happened to others, I have therefore recorded it as a misery.

V.26   Having escaped from a French prison, with a false passport, travelling through France without knowing the language, with a companion on your flight who speaks it fluently, halting at an inn on account of his being taken very ill and being obliged to feign sickness and to keep to your bed as long as he does, because if you move out, without him, or attempt to speak, you are sure of being discovered.

V.27   The misery of one of the *learned* exhibitors of the British Museum, displaying that depot of curiosities to five chamber-maids and three footmen on a holiday.

V.28   Being very liable to have your teeth set on edge, and hearing a person cutting a cork.

V.29   Having to cut open the leaves of a very popular book lent you only a couple of hours, and perhaps for the sole purpose of saving the lender the trouble of opening them himself.

V.30   Taking a walk in the garden of a friend with whom you are engaged to dine, unexpectedly passing by the kitchen and seeing the cookmaid chewing the parsley previous to mixing it with the butter for the fowls which you are about to have for dinner, by which natural process she herself the unnecessary trouble of boiling and chopping it.

The following misery happened to a most worthy and respectable friend of mine, and I dare say has not been confined to him.

V.31   Going to the House of Commons at an early hour to hear aninteresting debate, and being shut up in the gallery so long that a member below just rising to address the Speaker, palpably discovers that nature had triumphed over decorum above, and the Sergeant at Arms being sent up to discover the offender, betraying yourself by your blushes.

V.32   Loving to talk from the soul and hearing another tell a very long story.

V.33   Being pinned up to a door round the neck by the horns of an enraged over-driven ox.

V.34   A false calf shifting in a dance.

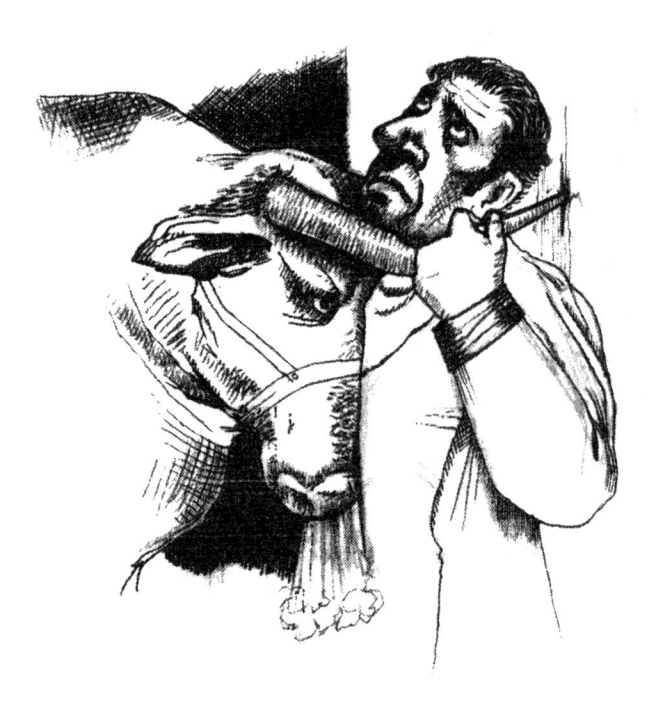

V.33: Being pinned up to a door round the neck by the horns of an enraged over-driven ox.

LETTER VI.

Fen-Lodge.

DEAR WHIMBLE,

I FIND that my worthy brother-in-law and his wife staid only two days in town, after which they proceeded to Brighton to spend the remainder of their blissful honeymoon. – I have, perhaps with the bitterness of an old grumbling bachelor, often regretted that marriage spoils so many of our fine young women, as ornamental members of society. Methinks I see a mark of arch amazement start upon your face. It is even thus: how often are all the accomplishments of an elegant young graceful creature, upon whom a costly education has been expended, suffocated in the baby-linen of her first child? After she once becomes a mother, the instrument upon which she excelled, is seldom unlocked, and the pencil with which she so finely drew, is never more pressed between the fingers.

My worthy Sister will derive no injury from marriage, for her accomplishments were solely confined to pickling and preserving, which I think are not likely to be interrupted by the laughing blue eyes of any tender pledge of love: although the silly woman, and I cannot help telling it to you (for I have just been informed of it by old Sarah, who mentioned it with a sly smile) actually purchased a stock of baby linen just before her marriage. I send **MORE MISERIES** – add, prune or exterminate as suits your fancy.

Ever yours,

F. MURMUR.

VI.1: Jumping in sacks at a fair and in the midst of the diversion hearing that a mad bull is coming down the street.

MORE MISERIES.

VI.1 Jumping in sacks at a fair and in the midst of the diversion hearing that a mad bull is coming down the street.

VI.2 An epicure in venison, being pressed by a party of twelve equally fond of it, to carve.

VI.3 At table after dinner hearing one of your children's little, but loud impromptus upon the lame leg or other deformity of one of your visitors.

VI.4 Being obliged to hear and applaud a vulgar impudent school-boy whilst he is repeating a speech from some play, at his mother's request.

VI.5 Also to hear very young ladies raw from school play and sing and to see them dance figure dances, without grace or agility, the poor things being ready to burst into tears at every spring they make.

The following misery, somewhat long, actually occurred to two of my friends, and I dare say may have happened to others.

VI.6 Going to a ball, becoming enamoured with your partner, procuring her name, and understanding that she was an only child, addressing the letter containing a tender display of your affections to Miss So-and-So, receiving a favourable reply, rushing to the house, being introduced to an *elder* sister whom you have drawn for a partner in the course of the preceding evening without knowing her to be so, who feels no objection to your person, and who of course concluding from the superscription that the billet was interest for her was disposed to receive your offer most graciously, being thunderstruck at the mistake, and covered with confusion being obliged in the most horribly awkward manner to explain.

VI.7 Walking with a wooden leg upon the Woburn Sands.

VI.4 :Being obliged to hear and applaud a vulgar impudent school-boy whilst he is repeating a speech from some play, at his mother's request.

VI.8   Having your shin scraped by a large powerful man going down a dance with extraordinary agility and energy.

VI.9   Being fumed with flattery to your face, by a miscreant, who you have reasons to suspect, speaks ill of you behind your back.

VI.10 Going to a house in the country, the people of which see very little company, also being put into the best bed.

VI.11 Overwhelmed with bashfulness, sitting down to a piano forte, to play for the first time at a private concert, the music book being only high enough to conceal your chin from the company whose eyes are fixed upon you.

VI.12 Three times pitching your voice too high, when you are asked to sing before a large party.

VI.13 Invited to dine with a family in the city, with whom you have the reputation of being a great genius, you are pleased at seeing one of the guests take out his pocket book and pencil, and write as often as you speak, you push all your brilliant puns and quaint sayings, after a little time you observe with *timid modesty*, that you ought to be very correct and happy in your observations, as you find they are to be recorded, upon which you are told the gentleman you allude to, is a great fishmonger, and that he is merely writing down such thoughts as occurred on business, such as "twenty-two salmon by the smack, Arabella, &c.

VI.14 The first day of a boy going to a public school.

VI.15 A girl at school whose feet have a strong natural inclination to turn towards each other, and who stoops prodigiously, undergoing the grace creating operations of collars, backboards, stocks, neck-swings, dumbbells and all the new instruments of torture in Sheldrake's shop.

VI.16 In the holidays being asked several classical questions by a dry learned old man, in the presence of your father and a large party.

VI.11 : Overwhelmed with bashfulness, sitting down to a piano forte, to play for the first time at a private concert, the music book being only high enough to conceal your chin from the company whose eyes are fixed upon you.

VI.17 A boy however naturally audacious with his playfellows, just come from school, and entering a room where there are six young ladies and no gentlemen present.

VI.18 Carving a very fine hot ham at dinner, and lubricating your thumb, and third finger with the fat at every incision, not to mention the almost inseparability of the odour which in consequence perfumes those very serviceable members of the human body.

VI.19 The horror of contriving how to adjust ones legs and arms at the age of nineteen in a drawing room.

VI.20 Getting the Caledonian Cremona[9] when you are just upon the point of marriage.

VI.21 Catching a violent ague in the first quartering of the honeymoon.

VI.22 Meeting a young lady the first time after your intended match with her is broken off (love tolerably, but not excessively deep) looking like two shy cats, each obliquely watching the other to see what degree of dejection the separation has produced.

VI.23 In the country asking a man whether he will have port or white wine, having only port in the house, when he gives the preference to white – No inn nearer than three miles.

VI.24 Listening to the criticisms and arguments of a learned lady.

VI.25 In a party to which a few days before you had introduced a very learned, but reserved friend for whom you wished to secure their favourable opinion, hearing a superficial elderly lady, who had the reputation of being profound, remark that she had examined him in philosophy, physic, and divinity, and could find nothing in him.

VI.26 Sitting in a gloomy small room looking into a dark narrow passage, the pavement of which is repairing.

---

[9] An allergic skin reaction caused mainly by oats.

VI.27   Going twelve miles to dinner, in doubtful weather, being anxiously tender for your horse, who has been bled the day before, upon your arrival finding your friend astonished that you had not received his note to postpone the pleasure, on account of two his children being in the smallpox and one more sickening.

VI.28   Going to a house where you expected to sleep, finding it full, pressed to stay 'till the moon gets up, which the expected hour is for the first time during its quarter, obscured by clouds and in attempting to get home by a short cut, learn of a cottager[10], whom you arouse from his sleep, that you have driven four miles out of your way.

VI.29   Feeling a violent irritation in your head at a dinner party, and being afraid to apply even the nail of your little finger to the peccant[11] part.

VI.30   When you are relating a narrative, which you only know superficially, finding all of your *little, and as you think successful flights of fancy* detected by a cold, crabbed disciple of truth and chronology.

VI.31   Going to town on purpose to receive your own dividend upon a sum which you understand is below the operation of the income tax, finding at the Bank a heavy deduction, and directed your appeal to the L—d knows who, and the L—d knows where.

VI.32   Being seized with a sneezing fit in going down a dance with a very delicate fine lady.

VI.33   Being a bad carver and notwithstanding every diffident effort to elude the office, finding the only chair vacant when you enter the dining room last, placed opposite to a tough hare.

VI.34   Upon a water excursion, drinking out of the same tumbler, with another person, and immediately afterwards discovering that he has an *unpleasant lip*.

---

[10] This term has changed in meaning over the years. So wipe that silly smirk off your face as here it merely refers to a Country Bed and Breakfast.

[11] The term "peccant" is an ecclesiastical one. It refers to corruption or being guilty of an offence.

VI.34 Upon a water excursion, drinking out of the same tumbler, with another person, and immediately afterwards discovering that he has an *unpleasant lip*.

VI.35 The weather looking very fine, volunteering to give up your inside place for the box, in a full coach, to a lady who is uncommonly anxious to proceed in the same vehicle, soon after clouds rolling upon clouds, and a deluge pouring down upon you – the coachman having only one great coat, and gallantry forbidding you to resume your place within.

VI.36 Losing the lash of your whip as you are dashingly driving in a curricle, for the first time, in a town where a fair is holding.

VI.37 Reaching a town late at night, not knowing that the assizes are holding there, no bed, or room.

LETTER VII.

Fen-Lodge.

MY DEAR WHIMBLE,

I told you that Mr. and Mrs. Debit staid only two days in town: they contrived however to display their taste by going to see Mrs. Siddons in Lady Macbeth; accompanied by our gay young friend, Swinburne; and they also contrived to exhibit one of the most vexatiously ridiculous scenes, ever performed before or behind the curtain of any theatre: poor Debit is very deaf, (and to have married my sister, I should have thought that he had been blind too) in the celebrated scene when that inimitable actress electrifies the souls of her hearers by whispering "out damned spot," Debit not knowing what she uttered, turned round to his wife, and loud enough to be heard in every part of the house, which was as silent as a tomb, exclaimed "my dear what does she say?" to which Dorothea replied, equally audibly, and forgetting where she was, "out damned spot, my dear" — Silly woman! Had I been there, it would have put me into such a transport of irritability that my nerves would have trembled for at least two months afterwards. Swinburne wrote to me yesterday, and told the whole story. All the people in the pit stood up, and every eye strained to see my rural sister and her cockney spouse; whilst bursts of "turn them out, throw them over!" resounded from the galleries. – I told you that they are now playing the fool at Brighton, and I shall dread to open every letter that comes from that quarter. Heavens grant the defect in Debit's auricular organ may occasion no more such horrible consequences. I have been fretful ever since I heard of the affair, and should be ready to quarrel with myself if I had not found a little vent in sending you a few more effusions from the school of grief.

Yours ever,

F. MURMUR.

MORE MISERIES.

VII.1   Miseries of a lady who being asked to dine with a very particular family on a rainy day, in consequence of not being able to get a coach, walks part of the way in boots, at length finds a coach and upon taking off her boots to put on her shoes discovers that she has dropped one out of her muff in the street.

VII.2   Going early in the winter to a coffee house to read the papers in which you expect to meet with some very interesting matter, finding the fire not lighted, and the waiters just beginning to rub the tables, not a paper arrived.

VII.3   Having made a newly-rolled gravel walk, finding some friends whom you had asked to dine with you, amusing themselves before dinner, by drawing each other in your child's chaise, which disastrously stood at the bottom of the garden, within sight, seeing the narrow wheels cut up the walk most unmercifully, and being deterred by a false notion of politeness from them a hint to desist.

VII.4   Being persuaded to put your finger into the cage of a parrot and to rub his poll *(see Footnote)*, upon an assurance from its doting mistress, that is the most gentle bird in the universe, suddenly feeling the sanguinary effects of its beak.

VII.5   In walking down stairs in the dark, coming to a forcible stop in consequence of being deceived by your expectation of another step.

VII.6   Going a bye way to a friend's house on horseback, through a number of gates, and finding the last locked.

VII.7   Sending a challenge to a man because you thought him a coward, who accepts it.

Poll - as in "Poll Parrot", a shortening of "Polly Parrot" which itself would seem to derive from the European "pollo" for chicken. However it could be "pole" as in "perch" as this is the spelling in the original text. Or it could simply mean "pole" as a rural term for the crest of livestock's head. Feel free to discuss this with a friend.

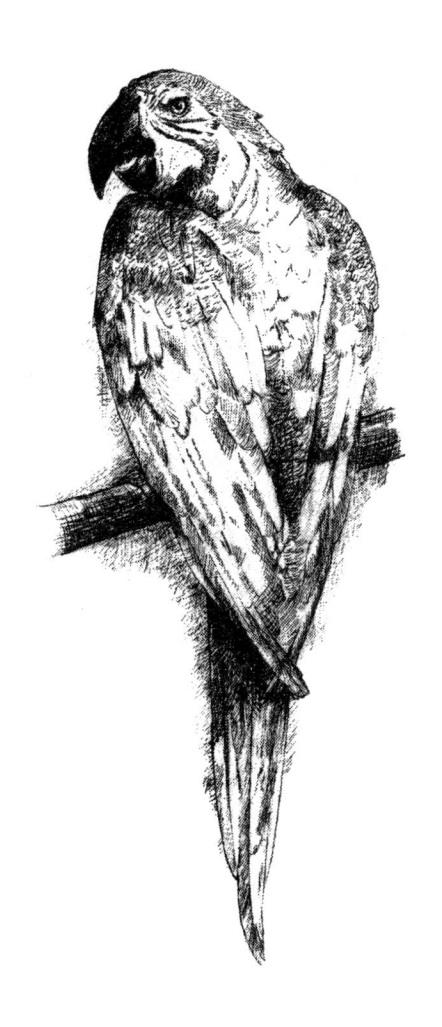

VI.4: Being persuaded to put your finger into the cage of a parrot and to rub his poll, upon an assurance from its doting mistress, that is the most gentle bird in the universe, suddenly feeling the sanguinary effects of its beak.

VII.8   Introducing a country cousin to your table, when you have a party of fashionables, and when the finger glasses are brought in, sweating to the bone upon seeing him awkwardly imitate the rest by driving his fist into one, and breaking it to extricate his ponderous paw.

VII.9   Knocking in the dog days, at the door of a house with a southern aspect, the sun in its meridian and the servant in the back attic.

VII.10   Buying a sixpenny bargain of a Jew who in exchange for a seven shilling piece, gives you a counterfeit dollar.

VII.11   Four persons in a room, three of whom are dotingly fond of whist, and the fourth not knowing the game.

VII.12   Your bad memory faintly flashing conviction upon your mind, that you have twice repeated one of your own jokes to the same person, at no great distance of time.

VII.13   Soliciting an acquaintance to assist you in a literary project, and being tormented by his diffident, disqualifying speeches.

VII.14   In a very rainy day, volunteering to procure a hackney coach for a lady, and after an hour's search, seeing one just come upon a stand, which is engaged by somebody else the moment you reach it.

VII.15   Listening to a man who is always aiming at being eloquent, is very fond of metaphor, which he confounds in the following manner. "As a mighty river, swelled by mountain torrents, over-running its banks, tramples under foot every intervening obstacle and fired by opposition gathers new wings from every impediment ; so oratory applied to our passions, fascinates our faculties, sharpens our capacities, and impels our judgements."

VII.16   Upon quitting the presence of a great man in his grand saloon, boggling at a false door, and forcing him to rise to show you the proper mode of your exit.

VII.17   Quitting a person difficult of access without having mentioned the only subject upon which you sought your interview, all owing to a long and profound dissertation on the weather, politics and family anecdotes.

VII.18 In the body of an interesting narrative finding a reference to a dry long note at the bottom or to some matter contained in the appendix at the end.

VII.19 Having fabricated a brilliant impromptu, which you felt confident would be called forth in the course of conversation, finding no opportunity of introducing it.

VII.20 Writing a play with infinite pains, every line of which you think unrivalled – and upon beginning to read it to a confidential friend, being informed that the same subject had been dramatized ten years ago.

VII.21 At dinner introducing a small fish bone into your mouth, and finding after an irritable search in your breeches and waistcoat pockets that you have left your toothpick case behind.

VII.22 Clerical misery – In preaching before the judges at the Assizes, finding a page of your sermon missing, by which you are left abruptly in the middle of a sentence which you thought the finest in your discourse, and plunging into the fractured part of another which has no connection whatever with the subject of the last.

VII.23 Half asleep and languidly moving to bed, pulling your chamber door after you with impetus, which you think will certainly shut it, and finding that the bolt of the lock has over-shot itself ; unavailingly fidgeting at the door, until you have lost all disposition to close your eyes.

VII.24 A family in the Country much addicted to scandal, spending a long day with you.

VII.25 Being in a great hurry, and attempting to blow out the candle with a long snuff, the same rekindling by the puff which was intended to have extinguished it.

VII.26 Attending a school play.

VII.27 In consequence of reading in the papers that the reservoir at Paddington would be emptied for the purpose of discovering a great quantity of hidden treasure, going thither with great inconvenience, and finding the whole to be false, being laughed at by crowds of people who were standing there and who had been deceived in the same manner – First of April.

VII.28 In the absence of your servant, lighting your candle with a match, and unthinkingly holding your head over it, and inhaling the burning brimstone.

VII.29 Shivering with cold in a coach the windows being kept down in consequence of two fat women who occupy the extremities of one seat being faint and disposed to be sick.

VII.30 The sensation of a school girl whilst she is comfortably picking a merry thought with her teeth, being angrily told by her mother before a party to hold her head up.

VII.31 Being sick at sea, and upon looking out of your wretched berth, seeing two or three passengers eating fat ham with a relish.

VII.32 Sleeping upon the floor in the cabin of a packet, a passenger above you suffering very much from the *maladie de mer* all night.

VII.33 Making sweet eyes to a lady without being able to procure one interesting glance from her all the evening.

VII.34 Hearing your friends observe of a portrait which did not do you justice that it was a likeness, but if they might be permitted to say so, rather flattering.

VII.35 On a short voyage impatiently and peevishly asking the Captain of the packet every minute whether the wind is fair and if not, when it will be so, and at what time he thinks he shall reach port, and having a surly discouraging answer to every query.

VII.36 Getting into a high coach upon a short iron step.

VII.37 Waking from a sweet nap after supper, having two stories to ascend to your bedroom, and a pair of new boots and tight pair of pantaloons to take off.

VI.36: Getting into a high coach upon a short iron step.

LETTER VIII.

Fen-Lodge.

DEAR WHIMBLE,

I have just heard from Brighton, and as I told you, Dorothea has been again making herself conspicuous. She must needs display her beautiful form upon a "Jerusalem poney," as the sorry animal, viz. an ass, is called, who kicked and threw her, to the great amusement of the idle folks who were parading the Steyne : and only four days since, Debit nearly escaped drowning in his struggles to resist the humane exertions of a large Newfoundland dog, who rushed into the water after him, thinking that he was out of his depth. —Really the follies and dreams of this new married couple are more vexations to me than any of the miseries I have sent you.

Ever yours,

F. MURMUR.

MORE MISERIES.

VIII.1 Wishing to have an early breakfast, and the kettle refusing as if by fatality to boil.

VIII.2 Having taken your place in the Bristol mail, being subpœnaed to attend the assizes the next day, waking at Coventry, having been put into a wrong coach.

VIII.3 A pimple itching so high between the shoulders, as to defy every attempt to relieve yourself.

VIII.4 A physician of delicate organs, called out of bed, to a rich, liberal, and irritable patient, stopped half an hour in a narrow street, by a night cart.

VIII.5 Walking in a dark night, without a lamp, or lantern upon unequal ground.

VIII.6 Awakened every half hour by the watchman crying the time, and finding your house robbed in the morning.

VIII.7 Going into a party, with a cold in the head, having left your pocket handkerchief behind you.

VIII.8 Calling upon a couple of dear *domestic friends*, and never finding them at home.

VIII.9 Having worn your great coat, and carried a large umbrella for six days, in consequence of the heavy appearance of the weather, without having any rain, going out without either, on the seventh, the morning being remarkably fine, and getting wet through.

VIII.10 Angling for the day, in a punt, with a companion who catches a fish every three minutes, without having *one bite* yourself.

VIII.11 Perspiringly entering a crowded drawing-room, struck with horror at perceiving as you steal an oblique complacent peep at yourself in the mirror over the chimney, a dingy, dirty line round your forehead impressed by the inside black leather of a new purchased hat.

VIII.10: Angling for the day, in a punt, with a companion who catches a fish every three minutes, without having *one bite* yourself.

VIII.12   Fond of being your own carpenter, attempting to take off a lock, the screws of which have rusted in their holes and your screwdriver perpetually slipping out of its bite.

VIII.13   Peevishly pulling up a window curtain, two pullies refusing to move, and three of the lines being twisted.

VIII.14   Seeing a little rascally bright-eyed mouse enter your chamber, which you have cursed through many a sleepless night, making sure of him, giving him a *nervous chase* all round the room, in very hot weather, he nimbly eluding every stroke of the poker, and after having fidgeted yourself into a high perspiration, seeing him take French leave through a tiny unobserved cranny.

VIII.15   Asked to meet a great wit, and placed at a distance from him at table.

VIII.16   A great and distinguished character at table, asking you a plain and simple question upon a subject, which you have written upon, struck stupid by a nervous awe and horror.

VIII.17   The miseries of a player who is no orator, being called upon for an apology for having kept the audience waiting.

VIII.18   A keen sportsman attending his second wife to the grave, and seeing the melancholy procession spring a brace of partridges as it enters the church yard.

VIII.19   At an inn going into a bed too short, with a wooden leg, which you were too fatigued to unstrap, drawing up the living one, going to sleep with the other sticking out at the bottom, which, when the chamber maid comes in for the candle, she conceives to be the handle of the warming pan, which she has carelessly left in the bed, from which she pulls you half way in a transport of agony, before she is convinced of her mistake.

VIII.20   Saying a good thing without its hitting.

VIII.21   Sending one of your coach horses, which has bad fetlocks, to the nearest farrier (a shrewd horse doctor) who pronounces this to be the *gutta serena*[12], and immediately administers a drench by copiously bleeding the hairy patient, and making him swallow his reeking blood, by which his life is endangered.

VIII.22 Awakened out of your first sleep, nearly suffocated by the stench of a candle just expired in the socket.

VIII.23 Hearing the bells ring for the marriage of your rival.

VIII.24 A person of delicate health to avoid damp feet takes a boat and after reflecting how nicely he shall escape a cold, discovers that he has been sitting some time in a small leak.

VIII.25 Being annoyed by the vendors of bills of the play, in going to the theatre, having a party of fine ladies to attend to.

VIII.26 Being stopped in a street, be some brewers lowering a barrel into a cellar and thrown down by dirty ropes, in endeavouring to pass it.

VIII.27 Having relieved a distressed object, seeing him *wink* to a brother vagabond.

VIII.28 An elderly proud prelate, sitting upon a settee, thinking that it has a back, leans backward, and falls head over heels, rushing to relive him horribly grinding one of his hands with the heel of your *new shoe*.

VIII.29 A great fop, who was afraid of spoiling his shape by putting any thing into his pockets, in taking off his hat to salute a lady in a crowded street, throwing out his knife, comb, toothpick, &c. &c. Forgetting that he had placed them in the crown of it.

VIII.30 A lady sitting for an expensive artist in the depth of winter, with her neck and arms bare to show her points of natural beauty, only for the painter to illustrate from memory.

VIII.31 Theatrical miseries – a tall fat man in dressing for Romeo, stuffing himself in a pair of tight small-clothes, made for a short thin person, and obliged to conceal the shortness of the waistband, by wearing an old fashioned waistcoat, with long flaps falling down almost to the knees.

---

[12] Also known as "Amaurosis" a loss or decay of sight without any perceptible damage or change in the eye.

VIII.32 Another – two antique amateurs playing Lysimachus and Hephestion (young lovers) in the tragedy of Alexander, in greeting each other, their Brutus wigs come off with their helmets, and discover their hairless pates.

VIII.33 Trying to see a pimple on your shoulder until your head grows giddy.

LETTER IX.

Fen-Lodge.

DO not, my dear Whimble, mention the French to me again in a favourable manner. The only comfort I have is in reading all the papers and works that are published against them: and though I trust I have as much benevolence as my neighbours, I really hate them as I do the Devil and more too. Every victory they gain shakes my poor patriotic nervous frame, from its extremities to the centre. I have dismissed my grocer (an honest man too) because he spoke well of them to my groom the other day, and have substituted another, because I was told at the club of which he is a member, he positively declared that he knew it to be a "*solemn fact*", that every Frenchman was made precisely the same as a monkey. From having been in France in my younger days, I knew that unless they were much altered since, this could not be the case, but the assertion proved the fellow to be so hearty in his hatred, that I cannot help admiring him amazingly, though I already find his tea has not so fine a flavour as that of his predecessor.

I heard yesterday from Dorothea who is still at Brighton, where she informs me she has received uncommon attention from a gentleman, who is there called "The Green Man," from every part of his dress being of that colour, and from his living upon *green* vegetables. I suspect that this eccentric personage must be a little wild, and will place her in some ridiculous situation or other, though she says she never met with a politer gentleman, and that he is much handsomer and better bred than our town-clerk. She adds that Mr Debit is very fond of him, for he seems so well acquainted with omnium and Stock Exchange matters.

I wish from my soul that this unaccountable couple would return home as soon as possible. Old Sarah hinted to me yesterday, that the sole reason which led her mistress to Brighton was account of sea bathing being favourable to procreation. I had almost forgotten to say that I have MORE MISERIES.

Ever yours,

F. MURMUR.

MORE MISERIES.

IX.1 Knocking at the door of a house for half an hour, and then being told by a neighbour that the house has been empty for the last two months.

IX.2 Raising a knocker freshly painted.

IX.3 Riding to visit a friend at a considerable distance, who you find set off at the same hour by a different route to call upon you.

IX.4 A thick short man waltzing with a fat tall woman.

IX.5 In a cold night putting your feet into a pan of hot water and drawing them instantly out upon finding it scalding, then as suddenly pouring in such a quantity of cold water as to neutralize the whole process - all the servants gone to bed.

IX.6 In a strange house drawing the curtains in a morning, and at one pull brings the cornice upon your head.

IX.7 Riding in a long coach very full, and being frequently tormented by having some small parcels taken out of the seat.

IX.8 Moving to get rid of a tallow-chandler[13], and the tallow-chandler immediately after taking a house opposite to you upon a *long lease*.

IX.9 A vain woman discovering the first blush of a large pimple upon her nose.

IX.10 A false tooth dropping out upon a card table.

IX.11 Tormented for a week with a severe tooth ache, going to a dentist who draws a sound tooth next to the decayed one.

IX.12 In gently elevating the candlestick to raise the expiring candle by a sudden jerk throwing the whole in a fluid state *upon the sleeve of your coat.*

---

[13] A candle-maker who makes his candles using rendered animal fat.

IX.4: A thick short man waltzing with a fat tall woman.

IX.13 Singeing your hair with your curling irons – ditto your fingers.

IX.14 A man writing letters to his wife and mistress and misdirecting them.

IX.15 Being nervous and cross examined by Mr. Garrow.

IX.16 In trying to recover your cocked hat as you enter the pit of the opera losing your party.

IX.17 Discovering in a large party, your name at full length, in chemical durable ink upon the corner of your neck cloth.

IX.18 Your servant out of the way, running down into the butler's pantry a house where you are intimate, and taking up the blacking for the clothes brush and smearing your coat from the collar to the cuff.

IX.19 Hurrying to a party and finding you have tied your neck cloth too tight.

IX.20 Being obliged to shave with cold water in the month of January.

IX.21 Sitting down alone in a large party upon a sofa which makes an *equivocal noise*.

IX.22 Playing on a piano-forte, miserably out of tune.

IX.23 Your memory failing in the middle of a song, which after two or three abortive attempts to get on with, you are obliged to acknowledge is impossible.

IX.24 Being requested to read a novel, to a party of ladies, of the style of which the following extract will serve as a specimen.

> "Touched by that *indefeasible* and durable impulse by which good and great minds are *gravitated* towards each other, the Marchioness of V. And the Chevalier U. Arose just at the same moment, when the high poised songster, with his downy plumage, was *winnowing the paly æther*, and whilst the hazy down still mantled the mountainous heights – at that hour *fermentive fancy* anticipated an endless plenitude of rapture. The roseate blushes of the Marchioness *kindled* the dew-bathed aromatic vegetation into lustrous animation," &c. &c.

IX.25 Losing your voice by a cold, being fond of disputation, and hearing an argument at table, in which you think you could take a shining part, whispering loudly, squeaking and sputtering, without being intelligible.

IX.26 Seeing a stupid fellow, half drunk, drawing figures with the wine he has spilt upon your table, which your servants have long laboured upon, to bestow upon it a *mirror polish*.

IX.27 At a party before dinner, hearing the weather discussed in all its tenses, past, present and future.

IX.28 Receiving a visit from a fashionable, with whom you have become acquainted at a watering place, at your lodgings in a court, in rather an ignoble part of the town, who convinces you by a half suppressed surprise of the latent determination of his heart, to cut you in future.

IX.29 Hearing that a woman who had lived with you as a maid servant, to whom you had ever acted with the spotless purity of Joseph, had sworn a spurious child to you.

IX.30 Carrying a sixpenny damson tart full of juice, in your hand, wrapped up in a thin piece of whited-brown paper, and carelessly thrusting your finger through the bottom of the crust.

IX.31 Having been promised a present by a friend, which he *never sent*, discovering from some indirect remarks of his, that he thinks *he has*.

IX.32 Landing in England far from your friends after a Continental tour, short of cash, longing for wine and fruit after dinner and not daring to venture on either.

IX.33 A man pressed to publish his friends for the first time, reading his work unmercifully lashed by the reviewers.

IX.34 The pantomime stratagems used on the Continent by Englishmen ignorant of the language of the country through which they are travelling ; for instance – Losing your way in the streets of Calais, not know a word of the French language, remembering that your hotel is at the Silver Lion, being obliged to put a shilling in your mouth, and set yourself in the attitude of a lion rampant, before you can make any one understand, and then with infinite difficulty, what it is you mean.

IX.35   No post day in the country.

IX.36   Engaging the attention of a large party to witness the performance of a trick upon the cards, and failing in the attempt.

LETTER X.

Fen-Lodge.

I have been tormented to death, my dear Whimble, since I wrote to you, by the agitations of old Sarah, who was subpœned to attend our quarter sessions, to prove that an old friend of hers, an itinerant fiddler, who was tried for having uttered seditious expressions, was occasionally disordered in his intellects. She has just returned in triumph, with a blue favour, having saved her friend, by proving that his head was frequently as *cracked* as his *fiddle*. Whilst under cross examination, William, my groom, who attended her, said that she made a lucky hit, which put the court into a roar : whilst Mr. Jekyll the witty Barrister, and as you know a *little man* in point of figure, who was concerned for the prosecution, was pressing her very sharply, the counsel for the prisoner, rose up, and requested her not to be alarmed at his learned brother, to which old Sarah, thus cheered up, took courage, and dropping a curtsey, replied, "Sir, it is not a *little thing* that can alarm me." I have often heard the old woman make dry observations, but did not know that she had anything like wit in her composition before. –Adieu, I have scribbled out a few more miseries.

F. MURMUR.

MORE MISERIES.

X.1   Interrupted in an interesting conversation by the thrilling notes of a very musical canary bird in the room.

X.2   Telling the company ironically, upon being pressed to sing, that they are to expect a melancholy ditty, meaning to surprise them, as you advance in the song, having the mortification to find that no one smiles, and upon the conclusion, overhearing someone observe, that it was certainly melancholy, but not so deep as he expected.

X.3   Snuffing out the candle for a lady, who is in the middle of a difficult sonata of Viotti – only one candle.

X.4   Getting upon a high stool or table to reach down a folio, and bringing down a cloud of dusty pamphlets on your head.

X.5   Going over a leap before your horse with the bridle in your hand, and finding from the obstinacy of the animal that he will inevitably pull you back again.

X.6   Turning your horse over a leap, letting him loose, and after running over four or five newly ploughed fields, catching him, and being so out of breath that you are not able to mount, at this critical moment seeing the hounds running in view.

X.7   A man being very fond of pantomimes going three times to see a celebrated flying leap that is over instantaneously every time whilst the trick is performing, somebody jogging him at the precise moment so that he is always prevented from seeing it.

X.8   Letting a new stick fall down the area of an empty house into which there is no possible entrance.

X.9   An amateur of executions, attending from a very early hour to contemplate his favourite diversion, the victim of which has to be some distinguished malefactor, and finding that the miserable wretch is reprieved as he mounts the scaffold.

X.10   Coming from a distant part of the country to London to see a grand procession, and overwhelmed with fatigue sleeping in the bed room of your inn and when you are awakened being told that it has passed some time.

X.11   Slapping the back of a supposed acquaintance in the street, who turns round and discovers a face perfectly unknown to you.

X.12   Two men with umbrellas in a narrow passage in a high wind.

X.13   Being fond of summer cabbage, chopping it up with great care and mixing in due proportions, vinegar, pepper, and melted butter, eating a great portion thereof and then discovering in the remnant three or four large green caterpillars.

X.14   Borrowing a favourite horse and returning it to the lender with broken knees.

X.15   Ditto, the feelings of the owner.

X.16   Nailing a deal box in a hurry, and by a violent stroke driving the nail so far that it splits the top in two – coach going off.

X.17   Making your thumb and fingers sore with pulling up the heel of a new pair of tight shoes.

X.18   Upon being introduced for the first time, in a large party, catching your toe in the carpet at the door, and consequently bolting into the room, as if you were intoxicated.

X.19   Riding a restive horse much given to hold his head very high, right in the wind's eye, a deaf companion talking to you, wind blowing sharp, hat rather large.

X.20   A young man much addicted to snuff, in a smart party, suddenly starting from his chair to take an empty cup from a lady, and dropping the attenuated secretion of his nose upon her beautiful white muslin gown.

X.21   Cutting your nail to the quick.

X.22   A man whom you have only seen twice, and know nothing of, who perspires very much in the head, borrowing your pocket comb.

X.23   The hanging committee of the exhibition, or committee of arrangement, placing an irritable artist's favourite production in a wrong light.

X.24   After have related to a company a piece of intelligence which you thought was only known to yourself, finding that they had been talking about it half an hour previous to your entrance, though they were too polite to interrupt you in the relation of it.

X.25   Obliged out of politeness to caress a favourite lap dog, which has sore eyes and bad breath.

X.26   Losing your shoe in the midst of a chase.

X.27   Putting a blister plaster by mistake to your broken shin.

X.28   At billiards missing the cue when you had the game in your hands.

X.29   Going into the country to a friend and finding the great wash going on, and lines crossing the shrubberies, covered with chemises, sheets, stockings, &c.

X.30   An interrupted sneeze.

X.31   Riding a horse in a hilly country on a hot day, and being obliged to get off every ten minutes to put the saddle backwards.

X.32   Travelling in a very mountainous country, with a horse so weak that you dismount him on the way up for fear of killing him, and walk him down for fear of him killing you.

X.33   Extinguishing the candle at a friend's house, feeling your way to the bed, passing the bed post with both hands, and striking your nose against it.

X.34   Turning a corner, being smothered by a gritty cloud following the first lusty strokes bestowed upon a filthy carpet.

X.25: Obliged out of politeness to caress a favourite lap dog, which has sore eyes and bad breath.

X.35   Losing all the gold out of a hole in your waistcoat pocket, and finding the aperture when you put your hand in, stopped up by a half crown.

X.36   Not being able to relieve a lady of her empty cup, by reason of having a hot full cup in your hand, which you are afraid of spilling.

X.37   Ascertaining after a week's unremitting agony that you must have your tooth out.

X.38   Going by the Gravesend boat – Newspaper wrong in the ride, by two hours.

X.39   Washing your face in the winter, chamber-maid having forgotten to put a towel in your room, bell injured and the lock of the door overshot.

X.40   Stepping the footpath into the road, the same appearing durable but proving to be villainous undried mud.

X.41   Rising up too suddenly under a large chimney piece after having carefully brushed the hearth.

X.42   Paying at the theatre in a hurry and being called back to change a bad shilling.

LETTER XI.

Fen-Lodge.

A ridiculous circumstance occurred in our Town, the other day, my dear Whimble : a celebrated Philosopher applied to our Mayor, for permission to use the Ball Room in the Guildhall to deliver a course of experimental lectures on Natural Philosophy, to which the sapient Magistrate with great dignity replied, that he would on no account, lend the room to any of them mathematical vagabonds, to have it filled with a parcel of *gim-cracks*[14] and *rattle-traps*[15] alluding to the philosophical apparatus of the learned applicant.

Dorothea in her last letter says she is promised a sight of the Prince's stables, which I am told do infinite honour to the genius and taste of the Architect Mr. Porden. She made me smile by telling me with accustomed credulity, that each horse has a Persian carpet to stand upon during the day, and a large mirror to see himself in, fastened over the crib. I suppose this is the silly prevailing notion. If she had been told that the horses wore pattens, when they were aired in dirty weather, to prevent them from catching cold, I dare say she would believe it. She has cut the *emerald Gentleman* I find on account of his eccentricities. A thousand thanks for Knight's enquiry into the Principles of Taste, it is an admirable production. Voila **MORE MISERIES**.

Ever yours,

F. MURMUR.

MORE MISERIES.

XI.1 Bursting your black silk breeches as you are playing at forfeits, and kneeling to a lady to call them.

XI.2 Not being sufficiently agile, or learned in the law of projectiles, to avoid having your hat knocked into the gutter by a sugar load being tossed from a cart into a grocer's shop across the pavement.

XI.3 At supper being placed at a separate table from the girl of your heart, trying to catch a glance, but always baffled by a provokingly intervening turban or cloud of feathers.

XI.4 Relating a disgraceful story of a man, his friend sitting immediately opposite you.

XI.5 Knocking upon some earnest occasion at a door with a small muffled knocker – no bell.

XI.6 The miseries of a very large lady upon being told that she has got very fat, after she had supposed herself much reduced in size, in consequence of having *screwed* herself into a pair of Mrs. Bailey's stays.

XI.7 Receiving eleven pence and half-pence in change at a penny turnpike, every one of which is refused at the next turnpike, a penny one also.

XI.8 Going into a china shop to lay out a few shillings, and overturning a complete set of very elegant china.

XI.9 A subscription at church, not a shilling in your pocket, a crowded pew.

XI.10 In a fruit shop in London, ignorantly eating strawberries at one shilling a-piece.

XI.11 Going to church when the service is half over, and being unable to open the pew door.

XI.12 Endeavouring to laugh with your companions at an accident which still gives you excruciating pain.

XI.13 Being followed by your terrier into a drawing room and before you can stop him, seeing him kill the tortoiseshell cat belonging to the lady of the house, who notwithstanding every explanation persists in thinking that you brought the dog for that express purpose.

XI.14 After kneeling , getting up at church before your time.

XI.15 Pointing out at a dance to your beautiful partner, the ludicrous vulgarity of a man, who she blushingly informs you, is her brother.

XI.16 Being seized with a bleeding of the nose, just as you have seated yourself by the charming girl, whom you have been waiting with the utmost anxiety to speak to.

XI.17 Making sure in your afternoon's nap of a large prize in the lottery and being roused from your reverie, by your servant delivering to you, a filthy, ragged, petition for charity.

XI.18 Walking in clean leathers down Ludgate Hill, meeting a flock of sheep, which have been driven twenty miles in a muddy road, one of which being pursued by the sheep dog, runs between your legs.

XI.19 The top of your teapot suddenly slipping off while you are cautiously dribbling its scanty contents into your cup.

XI.20 Springing up in a pew in the midst of the Litany in a fit of the cramp.

XI.21 In looking over Blackfriars Bridge at a boat, dropping your hat.

XI.22 After been entreated by a large party to play and sing, complying with their request and soon after being scarcely able to hear your own voice for the noisy prattle of the whole circle.

XI.23 Taking charge of a very small parcel, which your friend would entrust with no other person ; perpetually and nervously fumbling in your pocket to see if it is there, and unconsciously drawing it out, leaving it in the last chaise, and discovering the loss after a sound nap.

XI.24 Being told that a worthless old woman, from whom you expect a comfortable independence, is rapidly recovering from a violent and *very promising attack* of the asthma.

XI.13: Being followed by your terrier into a drawing room and before you can stop him, seeing him kill the tortoiseshell cat belonging to the lady of the house, who notwithstanding every explanation persists in thinking that you brought the dog for that express purpose.

XI.25 Being told by a friend that a review, the name of which he has forgotten, contains a handsome critique upon a book, which you have written, going into a bookseller's shop, and taking up a review in which you find yourself *savagely dissected.*

XI.26 Walking hard in a hot day meeting a *ceremonious friend* and not being able to get off your glove when he takes his off.

XI.27 After inveighing against red noses, discovering that the lady who sits next to you has a very rubicund one.

XI.28 Sitting on a chair which a servant has fractured and put back together the preceding morning, and upon attempting to lean back, falling to the ground before a large party. A country servant bursting into a roar of laughter.

XI.29 Whirling the cork off your float as you swing it into the water, and seeing it quietly sink with the bait to the bottom.

XI.30 Ditto catching your line in a tree.

XI.31 Ingracefully erecting yourself at a dance, bursting your braces, and your shirt appearing between your waistcoat and breeches.

XI.32 On a journey, both straps of your gaiters bursting, in bad weather. No boots.

XI.33 Talking loudly with a lady in a gig to prevent her noticing the unpleasant effects from the horse having eaten beans.

XI.34 Hot day – dusty road – long walk – tender feet – new shoes.

LETTER XII.

Fen-Lodge.

Mr. and Mrs. Debit are just returned to town: do my dear Whimble call upon them, modernize them, and put them a little in the right way of things, otherwise I shall dread looking into the Morning Post.

Mrs. Debit informs me, that she was taken by our cousin, old Lady Betty Worms, to a *botanical* lecture, at the Institute in Albermarle Street, I send you an extract from her letter.

> "I never attended anything so vile and abominable in all my life. —I had no idea the there was so much wickedness going on in the world, will you believe it brother? The flowers make love worse than we do, I blush while I write, and nothing can exceed the filthy and abominable disposition of the grass, that grass we always thought so innocent and wholesome, yes, the grass is more amorous, as well as I could learn from the Lecturer, than the goats ; not that I know anything about the filthy animal, only I remember that Thomas said one day when I was riding behind him, and saw a pair of them, that they are not virtuously given.
>
> This lecture is always crowded. Every seat was crammed to the very top - there were only five Gentlemen present, and such was the silence, that you might have heard any of the flowers the Lecturer held in his hand drop. If I could have got out before it was over, I certainly would, but as I was there, I thought I might as well was stay, and not make a bustle. I am sorry I took Eliza with me, she kept giggling all the time, although I spoke to her frequently. She has grown a fine young woman. I wonder the Society for the Suppression of Vice, does not inform against all botanical lectures: if these abominations are suffered, brother! It is no wonder that the French are permitted to bear the Germans"

So much for the prudish mind and just judgements of my poor addle-headed sister. I have heard of a curious fracas within our village which I must tell you of in my next.. - I accompany More Miseries with a brace of partridges

Ever yours,

F. MURMUR.

XII.1 Losing a considerable sum at vingtun[16] expecting to repair your loss by your deal, and being put out the first round.

XII.2 In shuffling, a split card always acting as a case to its neighbouring card, to the infinite interruption of the shuffle.

XII.3 Being only five feet, four inches, going to see a new play every part of the house crammed, standing upon the tips of your toes and only getting partial peeps at the stage through the misty glass in the door of the lower box, as a large pomatumed[17] head lolls on one side, and not being able to hear one word.

XII.4 Sitting down to play a rubber of whist, only one pack, and that short of its complement by three cards.

XII.5 One of the aces so terribly soiled that everyone can tell who has it.

XII.6 Travelling in ill health in bad weather, arriving at the inn and expecting to be refreshed by a comfortable dinner being informed that they have nothing the house, but they have just killed a pig.

XII.7 Crossing an iron railway.

XII.8 After having carefully finished the outline of a drawing discovering in the first application of the brush that you have been using blotting paper in disguise.

XII.9 Looking at an eclipse till you get a crick in the neck.

XII.10 Coming home late at night to chambers from a ball, finding your servant has absconded, and all the lamps on the staircases out.

XII.11 Discovering upon entering a drawing room by the disagreeable expression on the countenance of the party, that you have not been sufficiently careful either in walking, or wiping your shoes.

XII.12 Having caught a large perch pricking your hands with the dorsal fin in attempting to disengage him from the hook, the fish ultimately escaping.

---

[16] Blackjack. Ving tun – twenty one

[17] As noted earlier, pomatum is a scented hair oil.

XII.13   At the moment you are going to give check mate you awkwardly overturn the board – to add to your mortification you lose the next game.

XII.14   Turning your drawers inside out looking for a waistcoat, which you at length discover you have had on for the last half hour.

XII.15   Being obliged to kiss a remarkably plain woman at forfeits, when you engaged the pastime only with the hope of being enabled to salute a lovely young lady to whom you are particularly attached.

XII.16   A long charity sermon.

XII.17   Having a suspicion that your neighbours have purloined your turnips, hanging your horse at the gate, while you ascertain the truth of your conjectures, and upon your return finding that your horse has been made away with in your absence.

XII.18   Hearing a very interesting new publication read to you, and being obliged to wait for some time for a sheet to be cut open.

XII.19   Going to spend a few days with a quizzical family in the country, before your return, writing an account of their eccentricities to your friend in London, and recollecting upon your return that you have left the copy of the letter upon your dressing table.

XII.20   Being addressed by a man who is in the habit of putting his face close to that of the person to whom he speaks and discharging a small spray of saliva.

XII.21   During a general election constantly finding your newspaper filled with the effusions of electioneering gratitude, beginning with "To the independent electors, &c. Gentlemen, you have a third time elected me &c. By the noble exercise of your suffrages, I am returned to serve," &c. "For the distinguished honour you have conferred upon me, I return," &c. "I thank you for the great trust you have this day confided to me – I shall make no professions." &c.

XII.22 Female misery – near sighted, bobbing at a small needle to thread it, till you lose your temper, and at last finding its eye broken.

XII.23 Ditto going down a dance, and finding one of your garters every moment threatening to quit its post. N.B. said garters being Nelsonian, and having the following fashionable and high delicate motto on them, "England expects every man to do his duty."

XII.24 Dropping a new silk umbrella in the mud.

XII.25 Keeping an impertinent servant, who has been long accustomed to your habits, from apprehension that you change for the worse.

XII.26 A nervous man calling upon a surgeon and being shown into his anatomical museum.

XII.27 Upon entering a drawing-room, observing a coloured thread of worsted left in your cravat, which your washer-woman had placed there as a mark to know your linen from another person's.

XII.28 Peevishly speaking, unkindly of the girl whom you love to distraction on account of some little slight she has offered you, and finding that the person you speak to fully agrees with you on the subject.

XII.29 Having had a snug nap during family prayers, getting up in confusion a minute or two after the rest have risen.

XII.30 An urn, the cock of which you cannot turn, after you have set it running.

XII.31 In the country, a fine favourite greyhound of your friend, accustomed to jump in and out of a *ground floor* window, following you to pay a morning visit to a friend, who lodges in a *first floor* in the adjoining house, a child in the room, opening the window, and the dog jumping into the street.

XII.32 Dining with a very comical and irritable old lady, from whom you have some expectations, and in telling a good story, breaking the back of a neat drawing room chair, by an energetic movement of the body.

XII.33 Mistaking the sex of a great chubby faced female child when it's doting squeamish mother first presents it to you.

XII.26: A nervous man calling upon a surgeon and being shown into his anatomical museum.

XII.34 In a hurry to send off a letter, dipping your finger into the ink, instead of the wafer stand.

XII.35 At a great public crowded dinner, being placed over the grating through which several concealed charcoal fires send up their heat to warm the room.

XII.36 Going out to India, quitting the inn at Portsmouth in great haste, in consequence of the wind suddenly becoming fair, and when on board and under weigh, finding that you have left all the keys of your trunks behind.

XII.37 Having composed and learned a well turned speech by heart, in case your health should be drank a public dinner, finding all the powers of your memory melt away, the moment you rise to return thanks to the assembly.

XII.38 Also having made this eloquent preparation, no-one proposing your health.

XII.39 Having with infinite trouble, and some personal risk secured a good place in the gallery of the House of Commons, an interesting debate being expected, soon after it has commenced hearing the speaker explain "strangers are ordered to withdraw."

XII.40 Travelling – arriving at an inn to a late dinner, fond of pork chops, ordering some, when served up, finding them half done, and upon making a remonstrance learning that the cook had just put coals upon the fire.

XII.41 A dashing young lady just to town, for the first time, fresh from the country, to spend a fortnight, so bitten in the face by bugs, that she was not able to appear in company the whole time.

XII.42 In the stage box with a very genteel party, an old but humble country friend nodding to and incessantly looking at you from the pit.

XII.43 Reading a merry story, and no one laughing but yourself.

XII.44 Having precisely the same figures in your lottery ticket, as that which gained the great prize, but differently transposed.

XII.45 In cold weather, party large, getting a snug place by the fire-side, and soon after feeling the wind (a sharp North-Easter) cutting round your neck from the upper part of the window not shutting close, and curtains disordered.

XII.46 Entertaining doubts of the freshness of an oyster which you have just swallowed.

XII.47 Invited to a great public charity dinner, being told by your friend, one of the vice presidents for the first time, as the stewards are going round, to collect subscriptions that a donation of half a guinea is quite sufficient, and upon steward coming to you, putting said half guinea in the plate, observing him stop and hearing him say (the gentlemen near you all attention) "Sir, I am sorry to make observations, but" and covered with blushes and confusion, to find that you have given too little ; after fumbling in your pocket for five minutes, during which you throw out your knife, a key, and a small tooth comb, finding a one pound note, giving same, taking back the half guinea and wishing the steward and the charity at the devil.

XII.48 The sensations of a commoner and lady suddenly raised to a peerage upon hearing another pertinaceously addressed as Mr. and Mrs. So-and-So, before a large party, and an embarrassing apology following every time the blunder is repeated.

XII.49 Being much fatigued on your arrival at the home of a friend in the country, being pressed by his lady, with whom you are not very intimate, to walk out and see the country before dinner, she prefacing the invitation by informing you that she is an excellent walker, and that walk of four or five miles every morning does her a deal of good.

XII.50 Having received an account of the violent indisposition of a near old crabbed relation, from whom you have great expectations, going down to him with all possible speed, finding him in excellent health, and obliged to stay with him some time to prevent him suspecting the object of the visit.

XII.51   Thoughtlessly taking a piece of burning hot pudding into your mouth and keeping it there till your eyes water, a lady addressing you at the same time from the opposite side of the table.

XII.52   Attempting gracefully to hand a plate to a lady which is almost red hot, from the plate warmer.

XII.53   The sensations of a prudish tabby, who at an inn having undressed herself, stepping into bed discovers it previously occupied by a vulgar countryman, wide awake.

XII.54   At a coffee house, overhearing yourself unmercifully ridiculed in the next box for a work in which you had exerted your best powers, and upon the party passing you to quit the room, discovering them to be distant acquaintances, who had fumed you with praise to your face.

XII.55   Wishing to make yourself agreeable, playing and singing to a lady all night and being afterwards told that she has neither ear not passion for music.

XII.56   Dancing on an inlaid floor highly polished with bees wax.

XII.57   Being too late by half an hour in your application for a vacant living.

XII.58   Attending a party of ignoramuses who think you a great connoisseur to a picture gallery, begging them to admire that exquisite Guido, and being told by the proprietor that is a Rembrandt.

XII.59   Giving fifty pounds for one of the three Queen Anne's farthings, and afterwards meeting with half a dozen antiquarians who have one each.

XII.60   Speculating in the funds in expectation of a peace, and hearing that your ambassadors have demanded their passports.

XII.61   Being obliged to sit out the squalling of a silly great tasteless school girl, the mother of whom thinks she sings to admiration.

XII.62   Stepping with grace, and incautiously treading upon a cat's tail.

XII.63   An officious person always telling you in the name of friendship of every little idle gossiping story which he hears to your disadvantage.

XII.64   Constantly interrupted in your disposition to sleep all night in the mail, by the unceasing interrogation of a garrulous old lady.

XII.65   Having weak nerves, and hearing that a tin man has taken the next house to yours.

XII.66   Sending your servant four miles to borrow a book which you are very anxious to read, and after waiting at home nearly all the morning for it, seeing him return without it.

XII.67   After having been non-suited looking over the items of your own and defendant's bills of costs, which you have to pay.

XII.68   Being reminded every now and then by an old friend of a part of your history, which you would wish to forget.

XII.69   In snuffing the candle catching the wick too low, and pulling the candle from the socket.

XII.70   Dropping fast asleep at a crowded botanical lecture, and suddenly springing up from the effect of a frightful dream, and finding a constellation of eyes fixed upon you.

XII.71   Being asked if you heard Catalani.

XII.72   A man wearing powder, taking away by mistake your opera hat, you wearing no powder.

XII.73   Being a fag to a tyrannical boy, forced out of the window at night, to procure wine from the inn for him, discovered and flogged for it.

XII.74   After marching all day in the rain, and being obliged to wait till the next day for the arrival of the baggage wagon, before you can change your clothes.

XII.75   Having your umbrella turned up in a whirlwind.

XII.76   Going in half boots to a party and finding everyone in shoes.

XII.77   Passionately fond of the fashions and being obliged from prudential reasons to dress very plain to please an avaricious old uncle, with whom you come in contact generally four times a week.

XII.78 Over-persuaded to join a hunting party for the first time, put upon a fine hunter, and terrified to death during the whole of the chase, at the same time affecting to be quite unconcerned, to prevent being laughed at by the rest of the party.

XII.79 Being tempted to bathe in a romantic secluded spot on the sea-coast, finding on your return that the tide has come in faster than you have expected and irrevocably washed away all your clothes.

XII.80 After sitting long silent by a lady not knowing what to say, at least, just as you have manufactured a sentiment and having made the first ahem to utter it, hearing yourself anticipated by a person from the opposite side of the room.

XII.81 Hearing the best verses you ever made in your life, badly read.

XII.82 Cold day, getting a chair by the fire at dinner, politely offering it to a gentleman, who has a violent cold, and having it accepted.

XII.83 To be obliged frequently to meet in company a man, who opposes every remark for the purpose of starting an argument, in which he is always more vociferous than convincing.

XII.84 A first interview between a shy and reserved man, and one rather more shy and reserved.

XII.85 Walking in great haste in a hot day, and feeling two or three angular atoms of gravel in your tight boot.

XII.86 Being addressed by a man who is very fond of quotation.

XII.87 Asking a friend, whose digestion is very delicate, to breakfast, rolls doughy, no others being to be had.

XII.88 After a shower, sinking up to your ankles in mould, to gather a rose at the request of a favourite lady.

XII.89 At a pantomime, when the entry of devils is announced by a discordant crash of the instruments, being told by a man near you that he thinks the orchestra not quite in tune.

XII.79: Being tempted to bathe in a romantic secluded spot on the sea-coast, finding on your return that the tide has come in faster than you have expected and irrevocably washed away all your clothes.

XII.90 Being obliged to attend to a puppy that has an astonishing flow of words without any ideas.

XII.91 Riding to a ball in a new chocolate coloured coat, in which you mean to figure away, upon a great horse.

XII.92 School misery – hearing the arrangements for a pleasant excursion tomorrow when you are going to school tonight.

XII.93 Seeing old actors perform young parts.

XII.94 Seeing your dirty dog put his forepaws upon a crabbed lady's white muslin gown.

XII.95 Cutting bread and butter with a knife, the handle of which has been touched by someone whose fingers have come in contact with honey.

XII.96 Treading upon a cherry-stone in the street, day dirty – shoes slippery.

P.S. My dear Whimble, I feel I have a fit of the gout coming on, and I can copy no more Miseries for you at present – Adieu.

WHO IS SIR FRETFUL MURMUR?

Whilst there's no absolute evidence on this point, all our research points to Sir Fretful Murmur being a pseudonym for Sir John Carr.

He was born in Devonshire on the 6th December 1772 to a legal family. He had a sister, Anne Carr who became the third wife of William Hodges.

He went on to practise law at the Honourable Society of the Middle Temple in London. Illness forced him to leave and on medical advice he began to travel. His travels earned him an entry in the dictionary of nicknames and soubriquets as: Jaunting Car, a title which annoyed him greatly right up to his death.

A consistent and regular contributor to Annual Review he reached some notoriety with his first publication in 1803 of his poem *"The Fury of Discord"*. That same year his first travel book The Stranger in France was also published to considerable acclaim. The book featured several engravings and illustrations by Carr produced on his travels.

Sir John Carr was one of the first to visit France after the Peace of Amiens in 1802 when the borders were reopened. The illustration shows "Bagatelle in the Bois de Boulogne". Carr explains in the book that Bagatelle was formerly the palace of the Count d'Artois. He observed that the palace, much like *The Petit Trianon* had been let out by the government to a restaurateur. In the case of Bagatelle he says in true Murmur style: *"{these} Tennants of the government, who treat their visitors with good dinners and excellent wine, take good care to make them pay handsomely for their faultless fare"*.

In 1804 he published a play, *The Seaside Hero: A Drama in 4 Parts* which dealt with the threat of invasion to the UK from France, a concern at the time.

This lead to further travel books: *A Northern Summer* in 1805 which saw him travelling from The Baltic, Denmark, Sweden, Russia, Poland and finally Prussia; also in 1805 saw his best known work *A Stranger in Ireland* released. This book and stay in Dublin is most likely the catalyst for *More Miseries* and likely the setting for the real *Fenn Lodge*. His address given in the foreword is 2 Garden Court, Temple. The building remains and at the time was part of Middle Temple.

Wasting no time in 1806 he published *A Tour Through Holland* and in 1807 *A Tour Through Scotland*.

He was knighted in 1806 by The Duke of Bedford when Bedford was Lord Lieutenant in Ireland. He also received a similar honour from his Sicilian

Majesty: Knight of the Sicillian Order of St. George and Constantine.

In 1809 he presented a Book of Poems for and on behalf of Lady Warren for what appears to have been a charitable fundraiser. The Murmur style is never more evident in these verses than in the poem "Written in a Cottage by the Seaside":

> WRITTEN IN A COTTAGE BY THE SEA-SIDE
> In which the Author had taken Shelter during a violent Storm,
> UPON SEEING AN IDIOTIC YOUTH SEATED IN THE CHIMNEY-CORNER, CARESSING A BROOM.
>
> 'Twas on a night of wildest storms,
> When loudly roar'd the raving main,–
> When dark clouds shew'd their shapeless forms,
> And hail beat hard the cottage pane,–
>
> Tom Fool sat by the chimney-side,
> With open mouth and staring eyes;
> A batter'd broom was all his pride,–
> It was his wife, his child, his prize!
>
> Alike to him if tempests howl,
> Or summer beam its sweetest day;
> For still is pleas'd the silly soul,
> And still he laughs the hours away.
>
> Alas! I could not stop the sigh,
> To see him thus so wildly stare,–
> To mark, in ruins, Reason lie,
> Callous alike to joy and care.
>
> God bless thee, thoughtless soul! I cried;
> Yet are thy wants but very few:
> The world's hard scenes thou ne'er hast tried;
> Its cares and crimes to thee are new.
>
> The hoary hag, who cross'd thee so,
> Did not unkindly vex thy brain;
> Indeed she could not be thy foe,
> To snatch thee thus from grief and pain.

> Deceit shall never wring thy heart,
> And baffled hope awake no sighs;
> And true love, harshly forc'd to part,
> Shall never swell with tears thine eyes.
>
> Then long enjoy thy batter'd broom,
> Poor merry fool! and laugh away
> Till Fate shall bid thy reason bloom
> In blissful scenes of brighter day.

His final book, another travelogue, was published in 1809: *Travels in Spain, Majorca and Minorca*. The book was again illustrated by him.

This book, unlike his other travel books, goes into greater social detail and even includes a detailed chart of Spanish coins and exchanges rates. The social history is enhanced further by his trip coinciding with the Peninsular War. One of his index entires is reminiscent of Murmur with a simple: "Women, Spanish, their devotional coquetry". It was also during these travels in Spain that he met Lord Byron in Cadiz. Byron would later reference Carr critically in his attack on travel writing generally. While in Gibraltar, Byron wrote to Hodgson saying:

> "I have seen Sir John Carr at Seville and Cadiz, and have been down on my knees to beg he would not put me into black and white"

By this time Carr's popularity as a writer had peaked with *Stranger in Ireland*. The Monthly Review in 1807 (volume 54) rather mockingly put together a "how to" guide for a John Carr travel book. In their article they say:

> Without reluctance, we concede to Sir John Carr the merit of being a sensible and observant rambler: but he must be thoroughly aware that his pages contain little that is absolutely new; and that many of his accounts and anecdotes are in the predicament of the old lady's stories, which, though very well told, had unfortunately been frequently told before.

A vexation far from trifling occurred in 1809 when Carr lost a legal battle over copyright of his books. He bought a case against the author of *Right Merrie and Conceited Tour* (varyingly published under other titles such as *My Pocket Book, or Hints for a Ryghte Marrie and Coceitede Tour* and sometimes attributed to the author: A Knight Errant) published by Messrs Vernor, Hood and Sharpe. The jury could find no clear indication that the book was a copy of Carr's style or indeed his own prose. The court action attained some degree of notoriety in the US since Carr had by this time become very popular there. Later in the Harvard College Annual publication Salmagundi in 1926 the editor notes:

"*My Pocket-Book* appeared in London only two or three weeks after the publication of these '*Memorandums*' in New York — so that neither writer could possibly have borrowed from the other — and by its ingenious pleasantry and poignant satire, crushed a whole host of book-making tourists, with the luckless knight at their head."

His travels ceased when in 1811 he married a "lady of fortune" in Essex. Records are unclear as to whom he married, however his clear affection for Lady Warren around 1809 would imply that they were close. In his book of poems, the following is sent to her together with a rose and lily:

I look'd the fragrant garden round
For what I thought would picture best
Thy beauty and thy modesty;
A lily and a rose I found,–
With kisses on their leaves imprest,
I send the beauteous pair to thee.

His wife passed away prior to his death in 1832 which affected him badly. He continued to make the acquaintance of just a small group of friends, one of whom, the artist Richard Westall, provided the portrait for his book of poems in 1809. It is the only known portrait of Carr and is reproduced here with the kind assistance of Richard J Westall:

Writing to an unknown recipient in 1827, Richard Westall mentions Carr:

> I yesterday wrote to my friend Sir John Carr to express my regret that a particular engagement will prevent my having the pleasure of seeing him and you at Dinner on Monday, and to beg him to write to you to say that it will give me great pleasure to see you on Sunday next at half after five, if that day is agreeable to you both: and if it is not to request him to support another early day when I shall be glad to talk with you respecting the Drawing which you honor me by wishing to have.
>
> I am Sir, with great esteem
>
> Your very obedient svt
> R. Westall

Without a doubt this cancelled dinner will have made Carr's list of Miseries. However Carr also happened to be Westall's first cousin, so no doubt he was forgiven.

Following the death of his sister and her husband, Carr went on to look after their children.

Carr died July 17th 1832 at his home in New Norfolk Street, aged 60. An obituary in The Gentleman's Magazine (Volume 152) notes that:

> It is but justice to say that the light, cheerful character of Sir John Carr's writings was harmless, and that a lively and gentlemanly feeling pervaded his volumes. The plates which accompany his Tours are creditable to his pencil. Since the death of his lady, which case a gloom over his remaining days, he lived in a little circle of affectionate friends, beloved and respected.

His extensive observation of mankind had enriched his mind with a store of anecdotes, which in spite of his own occasional depression of spirits, never failed to exhilarate others, by this happy and humourous mode of relating them.

The connection with Carr and Sir Fretful Murmur is clear through the Miseries we have available and certainly in the prose style of *A Stranger in Ireland*.

Structurally it is broken up into nine chapters prefaced identically to *More Miseries*. The comma sees more action than the full stop and the spelling is similarly vague to the original text. This edition has indeed been corrected in that area. But while some of these spellings can be construed as "of their time", they are frequently identical: "pourly" for "poorly" and the overuse of the French "*recontres*" as though it were the only word of French he knew.

Murmur's Miseries also give hints of an early career in law, a debilitating illness early in life, being single at the time of writing, being a writer of plays, books, articles and songs and more over being a widespread traveller. Carr ticks all these boxes.

While these can be considered coincidences, it is curious to note that two editions of *More Miseries* held in the US both have "Sir Fretful Murmur" crossed out on the front page and "Sir John Carr" handwritten beneath. Also a copy held by a library in Philadelphia has a note to "file under: Carr, John".

John Carr is clearly the most likely candidate to be Sir Fretful Murmur.

ILLUSTRATOR'S BIBLIOGRAPHY & REFERENCE

'Fashion-The Story of Clothes' - Jacqueline Morley
Published by Macdonald Young Books 1999

'British History-The Georgians' - Edited by James Harrison.
Kingfisher Publications Plc 2007

'History of Toys and Games' - Peter Chrisp
Wayland Publishers Ltd. 1996

'The Chronicle of Western Costume' - John Peacock
Thames Hudson Ltd. 1991

'A History of Toys '- Antonia Fraser-George
Weidenfeld and Nicholson Ltd 1966

'Miller's Antiques 2005' - Edited by Elizabeth Norfolk
Octopus Publishing 2004

'Reader's Digest Treasures In Your Home' - Edited by Michael Wright
Reader's Digest 1993

'Newfoundland (Pet Love)' Angela Barlowe
Interpet Publishing 2001

'English furniture: The Georgian Period (1750-1830)' - Margaret Jourdain
Published by Batsford, 1953

'Wildlife, The Beauty of Animals' - Rupert O Matthews
The Image Bank 1989

www.periodclothing.co.uk
www.historic-uk.com
www.bbc.co.uk/homes/design/period_georgian.shtml
www.westlandlondon.com
www.elisabethjamesantiques.co.uk
www.findtheneedle.co.uk
www.denhams.com
www.museumofcostume.co.uk
www.sciencemuseum.org.uk
www.cardiff.ac.uk/news/archive/2003/art-meets-science.html
www.huntsearch.gla.ac.ukhttp://www.rcseng.ac.uk/museums/wellcome
http://www.thegarret.org.uk
http://people.pwf.cam.ac.uk
www.showhistory.com/anatomical.html
www.horses.co.uk
www.rcseng.ac.uk/museums/

With special thanks to The Huntarian museum

PRE-ORDER THANKS to

David Allen
Sean Brady
Mike Cook
Allen Dace
Alistair Dymond
Ben Dymond
Barnaby Eaton-Jones
Louise Ellender
Robert Ellis
Mark Frost
Cynthia Garland
Ben Hammond
Wendy Hammond
Rod Hedrick
David Hirst
Michael Hirst
Nick Long
Helen MacRitchie
Emma Mallison
Lizzie 'Lllama' Mellish
Sara Morgan
Louise Norris

Michael Ross
Ian Palmer
Elizabeth Pillings
Sandra Pleasants
Jonathan Potter
Susan Robert
Paula Scott
Emily Sharratt
Douglas Smith
Charlotte Soares
Phil Ware
Martin Welbourne
Gabriel Woolf

ALSO AVAILABLE FROM

HIRST publishing

A Dinner of Bird Bones

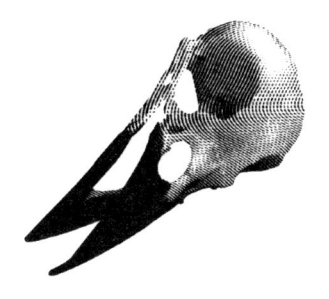

A Love Story
by Mr. Robert Hammond

———→◆←———

"A Dinner of Bird Bones" is the story of Lloyd Inchley; of heartbreak, new best friends, a girl called Atom, and how the terrible power of sudden new geometry links a mystery now and in the past – and how it is all witnessed by a presence that has silently observed the unspooling events for decades…

"A Dinner of Bird Bones" is a story about love.

———→◆←———

www.hirstbooks.com

ALSO AVAILABLE FROM

HIRST publishing

Lemon

by Mr. Barnaby Eaton-Jones

Spencer was an insignificant Data Input Operator and this suited him fine. However, when he is mistaken for someone actually significant, due to a mix-up by the Post Office, then his life becomes complicated. By complicated we're talking murder, sex, violence, car chases, beautiful women, and an annoyed fat cat (both of the feline and big business variety). Spence didn't like complicated things and he was as far removed from being James Bond as Shakespeare was from being a hack plagiarist.

A week in Spences life usually consisted of nothing more than dull, repetitive, time-wasting tedium. But, not this week. This week was going to be different and Spence wasnt going to like it one little bit.

www.hirstbooks.com

ALSO AVAILABLE FROM

HIRST publishing

Paddytum

by Mrs. Tricia Heighway

At one thirty-three in the afternoon, on the second Wednesday in May, something happened which was to change Robert Handle's life forever. At the time, he did not realise it would be a change for the better. Rob is man who has reached his forties without achieving anything at all. To his mother's dismay, he has dug himself into a rut so deep it will take more than a shovel to dig him out. It will take someone…or something, very special. Paddytum is the funny, poignant and heartwarming story of one man and his bear.

---

www.hirstbooks.com

ALSO AVAILABLE FROM

HIRST publishing

All Aliens Like Burgers

by Mrs. Ruth Wheeler

An exciting, funny adventure in space, for late teenage – adult readers.

Young, polite and intelligent Tom Bowler has barely ever ventured out of the small English town where he grew up. So when he applies for a job in a fast food restaurant at a "local" service station during his gap year he is rather surprised to discover that the vacancy is in fact based on Truxxe, a planetoid stationed between local galaxies Triangulum and Andromeda. Hes surprised further still to find himself becoming friends with a purple alien and that he has strange feelings for his android supervisor, Miss Lola. Tom soon discovers that Truxxe has many hidden secrets – just what makes it so special? And why is its terrain so rich and varied that it can be used for fuelling such a diverse variety of intergalactic spacecraft? What are the Glorbian space pirate brothers Schlomm and Hannond plotting? And just what is it that they put in those burgers?

www.hirstbooks.com

ALSO AVAILABLE FROM

HIRST publishing

Match Day

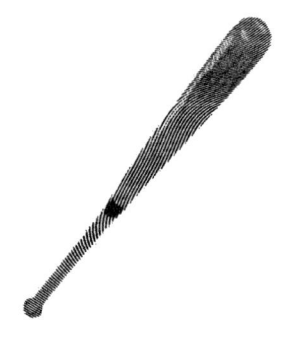

by Mr. Darren Floyd

A comic thriller about three people having three different days, on the same match day in Cardiff. Cathy is a woman disappointed in life when her dream turns into a nightmare, and mires her with debt which she doesn't have a hope of paying off. Suddenly she is offered a chance of a new life in Australia, but first she must take a desperate gamble... Martin is a bitter policeman with decades on the job, and a shameful secret in his past. He finds himself in events that he could never anticipated. Leigh is a supporter; he just wants to get into see the match. Unfortunately he gets split up from his mate who has his ticket. He finds himself alone in a city full of sports fans. Now if he can only find a ticket... Gradually these three people's paths collide, and none of their lives will be the same again...

www.hirstbooks.com

ALSO AVAILABLE FROM

HIRST publishing

Cemetery Drive

by Mr. J T Wilson

Death, it's a once-in-a-lifetime opportunity.

Alexa cheated death today. Well, at least that's what she was told, but how can you tell, if the Grim Reaper doesn't show up? Lucky she's got Robbie really, who'll go out and confront Death for her, even if it means going to the furthest corners of the world and killing himself in the process. And given Robbie's suicidal anyway, everyone wins.

Zan's having a bad day. Death's best employee, he's been collecting souls since the day he died, but today one wasn't there for him to collect, and that means a soul's achieved immortality and a serious threat to his job security. Now he's got to hunt that soul down and return it to the afterlife before the universe is torn asunder, before the fabric of space-time is destroyed and more importantly, before his boss finds out.

Featuring steampunk package holidays, demon summoning, sex, violence, casual drug use, possessed technology and technomagic of a universe-threatening nature.

www.hirstbooks.com